# 20 Lives Ignited

## How 20 Women Over 60 are Creating Success on Their Own Terms

Curated by

Linda Laird Staszewski

Aurora Corialis Publishing

Pittsburgh, PA

# *Advance Praise*

"*20 Lives Ignited* is a moving collection of stories from women over 60 who have walked through their personal fire and come out the other side stronger, smarter, and more in touch with themselves. Their stories are inspiring and offer a road map for others who are facing their own challenges.

"A must read from a sisterhood of survivors!"

Joan Roberts Hickman, President Hickman Roberts Production Inc.

"*20 Lives Ignited* is an excellent resource for women globally. Twenty women share their rich authentic stories of finding success on their own terms. There are endless gems in this book. I highly recommend taking the journey with these 20 amazing women. Grab your copy today!"

Joie Gharrity | Brand Director, Author, & International Speaker at Joie G 113

"'It's never too late to be seen, to be heard, to enjoy and celebrate life.' Heidi Parr Kerner stated this in *20 Lives Ignited*, and I couldn't agree with her and the other empowered authors more! These women speak from the heart, based on experience from 60 years of authentically living their lives. They have very real lessons to share and wisdom for you to learn from, so get your copy of *20 Lives Ignited* today! I have many coaching clients around the world who are over 60 who would benefit from these golden nuggets and insights for rising above cancer, divorce, financial devastation, and more. It's vital to look to others who have walked the path we plan to tread so that we can find our own version of 'the good life.'"

Dr. Shellie Hipsky, CEO of Inspiring Lives International, Exec. Director of the Global Sisterhood, and Global Empowerment Coach

"As a woman growing up in a very ethnic community surrounded by generations of Polish culture and heritage, I easily related to Peggy Schwab's inspiration of the impact of grandparents and parents instilling the foundation of dance, family, values, and assertiveness that would serve her well throughout her life. I found parts of myself in her life story and so many others who provided an introspection of the joys, challenges, discrimination, gender roles, resiliency, accountability, values, faith, emotions, successes, failures, strength, and honesty of life's journey!

"The power of *20 Lives Ignited* is that every individual will find themselves in the revelations expressed very honestly by the women who share their stories. This circle of women have shared their hearts and souls through this glorious journey called life, and it will give you validation that we are all weaved together as females."

Dr. Kathleen Bukowski, Retired Professor Emeritus at Mercyhurst University

"*20 Lives Ignited: How 20 Women Over 60 are Creating Success on Their Own Terms* is an insightful, compelling, and empowering read! If you are looking for inspiration and courage for meaningful change in your life, this book is for you!

"Twenty amazing women share transparent, relatable trials and tribulations and stark similarities that many women can relate to in their own lives, including mine. These phenomenal women share their struggles and successes, vulnerabilities, and victories. Each woman embraces change as their stories unfold with courage and transcendence.

"As an author, entrepreneur, wellness coach, motivational speaker, mother, and grandmother, I know that this book is a must for women who are ready to transform their lives with authentic gusto!"

Kathy Iorio Snow, Vice President, WellFit Incorporated; TV Show Co-host, Writer, Producer, *Wellsville*; Children's Author

"In this book, you will read about 20 women over the age of 60 who will share their story in a way that may impact and transform your life in a profound way, awaken dreams you may have forgotten, but most of all, IGNITE in you the passion to inspire yourself.

"As a speaker, magazine publisher, and author, I believe the answers to most of life's questions can be found in the stories we share. There are many seasons of our lives and in all of them there are opportunities to serve, receive, mentor, pivot, inspire, and grow both personally and professionally.

"I challenge you to read this book and make the choice to find the spark in you and IGNITE it. There are people waiting to hear YOUR story."

Patty Farmer, Marketing & Media Strategist, pattyfarmer.com

"*20 Lives Ignited* is just a wonderful read. It contains 20 stories of challenge, of hope, and of accomplishment. What a wonderful way to see that YES, I can too!"

Gary Glass, Leadership & Success Coach, Certified Proctor Gallagher Consultant

"Several of the women in this book helped change my life through their stories, support, and kindness. Their strength, commitment to supporting women, and encouragement provide a template for living your best life. Janet Kassir lived through a coup, where she found the love of her life, and learned to celebrate that you can find unexpected opportunities in life's trials. As an entrepreneur, she helps women feel great about themselves and developed a personal blueprint for success through hard work and passion. Heidi Parr Kerner has been helping women dig deep and discover their potential for years and provided me with the tools to recognize and reach for what I wanted in my life, including embarking on a new career that I love in my 50s. I loved reading these women's stories and found inspiration in each of them."

Marnie Mead, Former Journalist and Editor at the Erie Times-News, RN at the University of Maryland's Baltimore Washington Medical Center

"20 *Lives Ignited* is the powerful, emotional, gripping, and inspirational anthology of 20 mature women. You will fall in love with these women who have courageously faced life-changing circumstances: the extreme pain of loss, the wages of war, abuse, and serious health issues. Many may have collapsed under such hardships, but these ladies are overcomers, enjoying life with love and success, and now facing new challenges in their ongoing stories. However, now they face these hardships with confidence, resilience, and wisdom learned from the past. Events like those revealed in these stories cultivate godly, gentle spirits in our own lives and allow us to bring grace, joy, and love to those around us.

"As I look into the mirror each morning, I don't see self-esteem. I see soul-esteem. 'I can do all things through Christ who gives me strength'! (Phil. 4:13).

"We are women and each of us has our own story to tell. Each of us is special and valuable! Let's go out and change the world!"

Lynne Ricart, Editor for New York Times best-selling author, Ken Abraham

"What an inspiring anthology compilation! I especially loved the chapter by Janet Kassir. Her story is a poignant reminder that our life experiences—both wholesome and traumatic—are pivotal in shaping our destiny. It's up to us to use what we have learned from the people who have lighted our path along the way to forge a better future for ourselves. In turn, we can express our gratefulness by sharing our gifts with the world to light someone else's path."

Dr. Andrea Jeffress, Board-certified Physician Entrepreneur, Author & Speaker, Business Tech & Health Consultant

"Life is filled with challenges and setbacks that can either keep you stuck or fuel your success due to powerful lessons. There is an opportunity to learn and grow in every hardship, unleashing our passion and purpose, while helping us get to know WHO we are called to be in the world. In 2014, I experienced my own rock-bottom moment that fueled my own transformation and massive impact on the world. Now, my genius is empowering leaders to turn their deepest pain into their greatest power, this book is truly inspiring on so many levels. These amazing women have turned tragedies into triumphs, allowing hardship to fuel their success, help them discover more of their true selves, and impact far beyond themselves. If you're ready to tap into more of who you are, this book is the inspiration and motivation you need to turn your mess into your message."

Stacy Raske, Bestselling author, *Be a Boss & Fire That Bitch*, Founder & CEO, InFLOWential Leadership Mastermind, www.stacyraske.com

"The courageous women whose stories you are about to read have found their voice and their purpose by facing and meeting the challenges and adversities in their lives. In doing so, they share and provide inspiration, aspiration, and hope to other women as they travel their life's journeys, enabling them to find their own voice and purpose."

Joyce A. Savocchio, First and Only Female Mayor of Erie, Pa.

"What an inspiring and delightful piece about 20 fabulous females over 60! It was a great read, and I enjoyed hearing each story of their struggles and accomplishments. These amazing women are excellent models for us all and for generations to come. Congratulations to the awesome women of *20 Lives Ignited*!"

Jacki Cross, Co-owner of Brick House Coffee

"*20 Lives Ignited* is an empowering book for any women who is struggling to find her niche in a male-dominated world. I was fascinated by Peggy Schwab's story, in part because it is so totally different from my own. As a teacher for forty years, one could pretty much say that I never left school. Peggy on the other hand, directed her boundless energy in a myriad of directions. I marvel at her versatility and ability to grasp onto available opportunities.

"A number of my former students would benefit from Peggy's experiences. The story of how the little firecracker who beat up boys at recess learned how to channel that energy in so many positive ways is a true inspiration."

Nancy Bricker, Retired Teacher

"I have worked with, for, and have been the 'boss' of women my entire career. Every single one has a different and compelling story that shaped them. This book provided me with yet more examples of how great we women are. We all have those moments of reckoning that made a difference in our journeys. These are stories we likely would have never known had they not had the courage to share them. My goal has always been to find the best things in women that I know, and this book provides some insight into what women are capable of doing and becoming. In particular, Janet Kassir's story is inspirational, her response to trauma is smart, and her ability to share all is epic. Those who have experienced trauma often not only heal but rise to greater heights."

Elizabeth M. Costello, MS,CCC-SLP/L, Speech-Language Pathologist

"*20 lives IGNITED: How 20 Women are Creating Their Own Success on Their Own Terms* will not only bring you enjoyment but will inspire you. This is a book that might easily be included on your list of "Best books I have ever read."

"Most women could share difficult times in their lives. Things were dark, and we weren't sure what was ahead. The women in this book share their struggles and the triumphs that brought them out of their abyss to begin a better life. Don't miss this opportunity to walk the walk with these strong women and find ways to inspire your own journey."

Margaret Matthews, Former Reading Specialist at Gateway Schools, Pittsburgh, PA

"Reading *20 Lives Ignited*, and especially Tharifa's wonderful biography, reminds me we are all on a journey. Every one of us has a choice… and I chose joy. We leave a legacy of the people we have helped, our children whom we have nurtured in our faith, and my personal patients whom I offered hope in a chaotic world. I do thank Yahweh for giving me the tool box and the opportunity to face my trials and see the valleys as an opportunity to grow as a wife, mom, and friend. Without failure, the mountain top experiences wouldn't have the same impact, showing us that we are a blessed people! I can truly say that love was worth it all."

Jana Raquel Mullen, MD

"*20 Lives Ignited* is a compelling read and serves as evidence that the legacy of our past traumatic experiences may be overcome with persistence, enriching our lives. I especially found that true in Janet Kassir's story, as she recounted her time in the Peace Corps. Janet offers harrowing accounts of her experiences in Central Africa and Lebanon where she saw war firsthand. She used those experiences to inform and guide her daily life, which has allowed for a life well-lived along with a successful business.

"As a registered nurse, I began my professional work in mental health where I discovered the fragility and importance of mental health in our lives. I now work with hip and knee patients who also must learn to contend with and overcome the legacies of their physical conditions and maladies in the aftermath of their surgeries. The guidance and life lessons articulated in *20 Lives Ignited* are truly valuable guideposts to employ in my own life and to now impart upon my patients."

Kristen M. Rowles, BSN, RN-BC

*One day, you will tell your story of how you overcame what you went through, and it will become someone else's survival guide.*

- Brené Brown

# Table of Contents

# *Introduction*

## By Linda Laird Staszewski

My first job was as a server in a senior citizen's home. It was an after-school job. I always had a soft-spot for older people, finding them fascinating, and I enjoyed their stories. I listened to these people talk about their lives, their dreams and their regrets. I was just 16, but this made an impact on me. This memory was a seed for this book, watching some of these active, vibrant people light up with enthusiasm as they discussed their dreams. I was amazed by their energy, noting how much more passionate and joyous they seemed to be. They still had purpose.

Later, I started an office job, but I also worked a second job, as a cashier in a local supermarket. It was there that I met my husband of 47 years, the love-of-my-life, my best friend, my most staunch supporter, and my hero, Tom. I worked extra to pay down my first car loan. Tom is a year and a half younger than I am, so he was working after high school classes. We went to his prom together 52 years ago!

I wanted to be an artist and a teacher when I grew up. I was unaware of what goals even were, so I was without direction. After graduating from St. Benedict Academy in the business

Introduction

program, I worked various office and manager jobs. Learning to set goals later propelled me to help people with clarifying their goals, prioritizing such, and setting action steps to achieve those goals through my vision board workshops for both adults and children. I still strive to inspire others to live their "best lives." Ironically, I did become an artist, sculpting and creating, as well as a teacher, with my workshops and mentoring later in life. God is so GOOD!

After Tom and I moved to Pittsburgh, for over nine years, I attended night classes after working all day and earned my master's degree in professional leadership, organizational development. It wasn't easy, and it was a huge sacrifice, but it was worth it. I was given this opportunity and did my best to grow with it.

I started working as an industrial engineer technician, working up to being an industrial engineer, and then the plant engineer. It was challenging back then, as few women were working in traditional men's positions. I was resented, and it was painful, to say the least. There were numerous obstacles, but the Lord smoothed the path before me.

Creativity is a large part of my life, so after I became unemployed, after recovering somewhat from the devastating loss of the job, I went through depression and anxiety and decided it was time to reinvent myself, to "Let go and let God." First, Escape to Create Workshops was born, which included vision boards, everyone's favorite. Then came DIY Crafts Kit subscriptions, followed by Queens Comfort Boxes, (personalized gift boxes). I started a Facebook group, "Unwavering Women 60+: Live Your Best Life," where women could connect, learn, and share. I so understood the glass ceiling and inequities that women were up against. I wanted to offer support and connection to other women.

I have always wanted to write a book. And like so many others, I started a book and it never materialized. When I learned of the anthology concept, I wanted in! When I was unable to find one, I turned to prayer. I felt the Lord tap me on the shoulder and say, "Why not you?" I listened, and I dove in!

So that's when I set out on this journey to make *20 Lives Ignited: How 20 Women Over 60 are Creating Success on Their Own Terms.*

My anthology features 20 strong, amazing women who have overcome obstacles in their lives to become their own success stories. Our mission is to be an inspiration and motivate girls, women of all ages, and especially women over the age of 60. We want everyone to know that you're never too old, and it is never too late. We've only just begun at age 60! I am now 71! I have so many goals for the future, so many projects, and I live a life of pure joy and gratitude!

Introduction

Each chapter of *20 Lives Ignited* features a woman's personal story of triumph. Some themes may include stories about horrifying marriages and a woman surviving abuse. Others are more mellow, where a woman reinvents herself, or is on a journey toward finding herself and her purpose.

These authors, who I am so proud to be connected with, have proven that women over 60 are valuable assets to society and to communities everywhere. They are wise, knowledgeable, courageous, powerful, creative, and beautiful! And, we have only JUST BEGUN!

So, I encourage you to learn HOW these 20 women did it! I believe you will be pleasantly surprised about these amazing women and their captivating stories.

We follow our dreams, and we are UNSTOPPABLE! All glory to God. Create your own success! If we can do it, so can you!

# A Ray of Light

## Women who Inspire

# *Thrive*

## Sydney Amicucci MEd, MHt, MRt

"We are on a most fascinating journey of self-discovery. Live, learn, and thrive!"

- Sydney Amicucci

Your journey is most likely similar to mine in many aspects. We all experience a huge range of emotions, lots of ups and downs, and you may have asked yourself, "What is my purpose? Who am I? Where am I going from here?"

As we progress through the stages of life, from birth to adulthood, it is difficult to imagine we once were a bundle of cells in the womb—complete with our own unique DNA. We were like an open book with the chapters of our lives just waiting to unfold. My journey has been wrought with extreme challenges. Some of those challenges resulted in a 180-degree shift in the direction of who I thought I was and who I became.

At age 36, I was a wife and a mother of three curious, fun-loving, and creative boys. My career as an educator, counselor,

1

and future principal was set. Already an adjunct professor, opportunities automatically landed in my direction. I jumped at every opportunity that arose, eager to excel and prove myself.

As a soccer mom, I helped with school fundraisers and was asked by the school district to be the main director for the planning committee in charge of the yearly carnival fundraiser. Being passionate and an idea generator, I always strove to do the best job I could and be the best version of myself. I had been taught from a young age by my parents to always do my best and to compete with myself. My parents were loving, diligent, honest, caring, passionate people, and extremely hard working. Their example instilled those same ethics in me, but amid all the planning and effort, life can have a way of pulling the rug out from under you!

I was a vice principal in charge of activities and discipline. While completing a grant project on my computer at school, the letters and lines began to dance as if doing the Latin Macarena, and I began to stumble and intermittently bump full-on into door jambs. Physical warnings were alerting me that something was horribly amiss. In my career, I was a Type-A personality to the max! Figuring I could handle about anything in life, I simply forged ahead and continued to ignore the alerts. I'd rationalize that I was just overworked, tired, and needed a vacation. So, I continued to push through. Not a good idea!

Looking back, I know that pushing through and overworking were dysfunctional ways of self-medicating. Being an overachiever had become a way of life for me, starting in childhood. Striving to prove myself, being a people pleaser, and making sure not to create waves or cause disharmony became an integral part of my personality. The expectations I put upon myself were unrealistic. As an adult, I attempted to be perfect as a wife, mother, and educator. That is an impossible goal to achieve. We do not live in a perfect world and striving for total perfection leads to disaster!

As children, my three sons were, and still are, my pride and joy. Ryan (11 years old), Scott (eight years old), and Kenny (six months old) were all close, intuitive, and exceptionally bright. Parenthood has been a true gift, but my marriage was beyond help or repair. My husband was an alcoholic. Anyone who lives with an alcoholic knows the direct ravages the disease reaps ... on everyone. My husband refused to seek treatment. He would drink after the workday and well into the night. Then, as the alcohol overtook his inhibitions, he would easily slip into a rage and was tormented by bouts of anger and depression. Alcoholism is vicious, and I believe the disease takes over the person eventually leaving them terribly wounded and emotionally twisted.

I attended Al-Anon meetings. The meetings were helpful, and they provided insight along with various resources for help. I learned about the three *Cs*. With any substance abuse, family

3

members learned that we did not *cause, cure,* or *control* the addiction. I knew hope was lost in saving the marriage. My sons and I had endured so much pain and sorrow. The sorrow cut so deeply into my heart and soul that I felt like the core of my being was dying, and I was filled with shame. I had to find a safe way to leave with my sons. At that same time, my husband was released from his job, and his anger escalated.

Any outsider would believe we were the *perfect* family — beware of smokescreens! Seriously, there is no such thing as a *perfect* family. The stress of attempting to hold everything together was unbearable. Frequent migraines, vertigo, and the inability to sleep soundly led me to seek medical attention. I was referred to a neurologist. The neurologist informed me that I had completely overextended myself. The tremendous amount of stress had a huge toll on my health. Results of the tests in 1989 revealed that my brain and body were compared to an unhealthy 70-year-old female. Everything in my brain, body, and emotions seemed like an aberration. I was betrayed by my own body.

Feeling flushed and confused, I was in a state of disbelief. I allowed myself to become stretched to the limit physically, emotionally, and mentally, and I was short-circuiting. The nurse attempted to console me. She was like my guardian angel. I leaned into her and then felt myself slip away. I had coded! My life changed forever at 36 years old.

Near-death experiences change a person's perceptions about life and death. The synchronicity of standing by *my angel nurse* had saved my life. Basil Artery Dysfunction (BAD) was the culprit. The basilar artery directly supplies blood to the brainstem and cerebellum. When the basil artery shuts down, *boom*, death can be imminent!

A *blur* describes the next few years of my life which consisted of physical rehabilitation, learning to walk, forming new neural pathways, and attempting to repair a screwed-up brain. Gut-wrenching sobs rendered me completely exhausted much of the time. My soul was wounded. I yearned to hug and hold my boys. Every task seemed to be monumental. I was *angry* at life and at God! Through flowing tears, I asked God, *why me?* The response was compassionate, loving, and supportive. I actually heard, *why not?* Understanding came with that response—we are spiritual beings with a body, and there are many lessons to learn. Healing began.

Resounding deep within, there was renewed hope—a knowing that I was being uplifted in ways I cannot even describe. Lucid dreams and messages became commonplace. I still have some lingering health challenges, and life is full of ups and downs, but I have discovered that all experiences have a purpose.

Eventually, as I grew stronger the marriage ended. A new beginning. Healing myself and others became my major goal. Messages flooded my thoughts. I began to work with children and adults who had experienced trauma. I immersed myself in classes and training to become a mental health counselor, spiritual advisor, trauma therapist, and writer. I used the guidance and what I experienced to become more self-actualized and to have a deeper understanding so others could obtain hope. I stepped out in faith. It sounds easy, but it wasn't. It isn't!

Opportunity knocks in a myriad of ways. I've always been a spiritual person. As a child, I'd talk to God and my angels. I still do. Sometimes I even yell at them, like a child. I wait, pay attention, work at staying present, and allow trust and my intuition to be of support. I pray, seek insight, and I use the gifts God bestowed upon me. We all have gifts; that's right, you have many gifts you might not have even thought about.

The Holy Bible provides us with insight. Peter spoke of spiritual gifts, and among the gifts are prophecy, ministering, wisdom, knowledge, faith, healing, teaching, exhorting, giving, ruling, and interpreting. And *love*. Think about your gifts; use them. They are meant to be shared.

In 1999, my physician recommended I learn hypnosis to help me heal. My goals were to help more people, to become stronger, calmer, stay more focused, and to sleep better. Through the transpersonal hypnotherapy classes, I learned how to tap into my own unlimited potential more effectively, to reframe thinking, and to become more productive without burning myself out. With a new lease on life, I was led to become a statewide master level transpersonal hypnotherapist through the National Association of Transpersonal Hypnotherapy (NATH)—a mind, body, spirit approach. I was hired by doctors to help train others in the field of hypnotherapy and to write individualized scripts for each client. By 2000, I had opened my own hypnotherapy and wellness business, INNERventions. I call it that because so much of what we do to heal is *inner* work.

I have been blessed to help thousands of people and share in everyone's unique and incredible story. I offer group and individual hypnotherapy, spiritual readings, and energy work. Since 1999, I have also been published in *Script Magic* and *Whole Life health* magazines and have taught hypnosis and neurolinguistics classes. I'm still a statewide consultant and trainer in the field of hypnotherapy.

In 2009, I met the love of my life, Frank Amicucci. He is my best friend, my rock, and my husband. You are never too old to love again. We work side-by-side writing together, providing hypnotherapy, and offering classes and sessions in self-hypnosis, health and wellness, regressions, meditation, mindfulness, and Reiki.

It is vital for people to realize we can move forward regardless of our challenges. We have resilience in our thinking and actions. For over 20 years, I've stated that we are attending what I call *earth school*. Lessons are difficult as well as enlightening. Life includes a smattering of delightful, loving, insightful, and creative people, events, and opportunities that have the potential to uplift and carry us during every stage of life. When we achieve something good, it is a team effort. Never underestimate your worth or ability to help yourself or others. Each day is a new beginning—a blank page waiting for you to write on—to create, grow, understand, and focus on the positives, as well as possibilities.

We can elect to view our experiences with hope and vitality. Focus on what you can do, on how to help yourself and others, and on reaching out to one another. Above all, live with compassion and love. Learn to love yourself, flaws and all. When we lead others to excel and to heal, we all win. We continue to be on our journey together. Know that you are loved ... unconditionally!

## About Sydney

Sydney is the owner of INNERventions, a transpersonal hypnotherapy and wellness (mind, body, spirit) practice since 2000. As a published writer, her topics include spiritual, metaphysical, and transpersonal hypnotherapy. Additionally, Sydney was associated with Nova Spiritus (Sylvia Browne) study groups. She is an evidential intuitive reader and a medical empath (since childhood). She is a retired multi-systemic therapist (MST) and trauma-focused care therapist, alternative education counselor, and director and adjunct college professor in psychology, sociology, dynamic communications, and master-of-education programs.

Professional training includes certification as a master-level transpersonal hypnotherapy facilitator and statewide educator with the National Association of Transpersonal Hypnotherapy (NATH) since 1999. Sydney has a degree in psychology and a master's degree in educational psychology. Training and experience have provided the opportunity to offer classes and sessions that help people manifest their goals, improve thinking, create a healthier and happier life, as well as optimizing potential. Sydney is a skilled regression facilitator for the journey of past-life regression, future-life progression, and life-between-life sessions. Ongoing classes include Discovering Your Gifts, Meditation, Reiki, Dream Interpretation, and circle groups to learn and practice Tarot along with how to provide intuitive readings.

**Connect with Sydney**

https://innerventionswellness.com/

# It's Your Time to SHINE!

## Heidi Parr Kerner

"Find the courage to grow into the person you've always envisioned yourself becoming."[1]

- Meggan Roxanne

## GROCERY STORE. SATURDAY MORNING.

## AISLE1: PRODUCE

I was running around doing last-minute errands preparing to have guests for dinner that evening. I noticed an attractive woman walking toward me, smiling and waving. Geez, I thought,

---

[1] Roxanne, Meggan. https://psychology-daily.tumblr.com/post/648961402496778240/psychology-app-learn-grow-and-improve-yourself

*who is she?* I didn't have my glasses on. As she approached the fresh food section, she seemed genuinely happy to see me. It clicked, Carol. Help! Not today. As a successful member of the community, I knew her casually from shared business affiliations. I smiled, waved, and briskly moved on with my fresh salad items in tow. Extending pleasantries with her was always daunting. "Business is slow. I'm feeling unwell. The weather doesn't help. My cat just died." She would rattle on; her facial expressions showing little affect. Frankly, I felt she was depressed.

## AISLE 7: CONDIMENTS

Placing a bottle of sunflower basting oil in my grocery cart there was Carol standing next to me obviously delighted by our chance encounter. I'll say this for her, she is one determined lady. I noticed something different about her. Not a woman recognized for style, Carol looked stunning. A bright and bold silk floral blouse over black fitted slacks, tall leather boots, and a large matching handbag. Her hair tied attractively in a chignon. A sparkle in her eyes. Her voice was animated. I must admit, I was fascinated by her transformation.

"Carol," I began. "I love your blouse. It's fabulous. You go, gal. You look absolutely wonderful!" And I sincerely meant it. Her face revealed pleasure from the compliment. "I've a little secret I'll share with you," she replied. Clutching my grocery list in hand and moving on to the next aisle, what came next was a surprise to me.

"I never wear anything so dramatic as you see me in today. But this morning when I awoke springtime was in the air, and I felt a deep inner voice whispering, *Get out of shy you, Carol. Do something wild!*" In a voice tinged with the naughtiness of a little girl sharing a secret, she continued, "I bought this blouse two years ago but when I brought it home, I felt it was *too over the top* for me." An impish smile framed her face much like a child stealing a cookie from a cookie jar.

"I was very close to my grandmother who influenced me greatly. As a little girl, she always instilled in me that children should be seen but not heard, never draw attention to oneself, be modest, don't brag, stay in the background." Her words brought me to a sudden halt as she continued "If she saw me dressed as I am today, she would turn over in her grave." Her words had captured my full attention. I felt she wanted more from me at this moment. Standing before me she was definitely out of her comfort zone.

"Seeing the new you today, Carol—your style, your lightness of mood—feeling your joyful spirit is heartwarming. Why not do this more often?" She looked mystified. "Absolutely not, Heidi! I'm in my late 60s. It's too late for me to change."

I added, "Oh Carol, it's never too late to change."

Carol had taken her dear grandmother's words to heart. They had falsely impacted her life forever. Words wound. So many years ago, a frightened little girl retreated to a forced reality within.

Carol, although not a participant, was familiar with members of my various women's empowerment programs. She said, "I love seeing other women playing bigger. It inspires me—their dedication to personal and professional growth and encouraging one another." As an afterthought, she added, "Their clothing styles, outlandish jewelry, and their involvements. Fun activities. I see them reach out of their comfort zones. But it's not for me. I'm really okay being in the background."

Only being in the background? Was she really? I was getting mixed messages.

I asked how she was feeling today as she presented her new persona. Shyly she responded, "It's uncomfortable. But I like it."

Even though Carol was successful in her business, I knew another creative part of her wanted to be unleashed.

Intuitively, I felt Carol's early creative life had been stifled. "It's never too late," I again emphasized. "It's never too late to be seen, to be heard, to enjoy and celebrate life. Do you remember the dreams of that little girl within? I believe she's alive and well and only waits for you to call her name."

## CHECK OUT

At last!

Finally arriving at checkout (I was running late), Carol, laughingly, sang out her parting words, "Remember, Heidi, it's only for today. Only for today." And she happily danced off to the bakery section.

\* \* \*

Carol represents innumerable women I have coached through the years who, for whatever reason, have shut down. Education, careers, raising families, relationships. They've gotten busy. Yet, oftentimes, beneath it all, there remains a yearning for *something more.*

Like Carol, they feel it's too late. There is a part of them that is unhappy. Who are they to play bigger? To dare to be different? They often are on the shy or introverted side, and yet there's a part of them that would like to step out and shine. But how do they do that? Where do they do that, and what would people think if they did do that?

Regardless of age, I believe all women have a purpose in life. No matter what the age, I believe it's so important to step out of one's comfort zone, address apprehension, seek other like-minded women, and shine like the sun! How do I know this? Because I did it.

How did I go from being so withdrawn around strangers to pursuing a career that places me in the limelight? To be a motivational speaker, coaching corporate executives, producing and acting in community theater, and to be acknowledged as a leader in my community? I made a conscious decision. I needed to transcend my inferiority and become the person I longed to be.

I was a painfully shy little girl who yearned for more. My mission and my true passion in my current role as the leader of The Coffee Club Divas (a women's professional networking organization) is to enable other women to discover their own unique gifts leading them to a more authentic, joyful, and fulfilling life.

I was raised the oldest of six children in a strong Catholic family: my dad a successful banker, my mom a homemaker. As in Carol's upbringing, our household adhered to the generational adage that children be seen and not heard.

However, I possess a fanciful imagination. My home was my stage, where I wore the mantle of creative leadership in theatrical productions, dramatic monologues, dancing and singing, and even orchestrating a carnival for muscular dystrophy. With a cast of five younger siblings and select neighborhood children, I was a serious and demanding director by age12.

But outside the safety of my home, I retreated into shyness and silence. There was a boy at my bus stop, Ben, who was my age. I stood next to Ben for three years and never spoke to him. Each morning my mother would urge me, "Please, Heidi, just say 'hello'." She begged, "Please, just try. I'll give you a dollar!"

Yet I stood, stoically, praying for the bus to arrive without uttering a word to Ben.

In school, my teachers described me as a cooperative child, but quiet and hesitant to participate in discussions.

I was the nerdy girl in school. Picked last for team sports. Bullied by my peers. Very few friends. I longed to be one of the popular girls I envied. They walked into the room confident. The girls wanted to be their friends. The boys wanted to go steady with them.

My father came home and announced we'd be moving to Erie, Pennsylvania, due to a bank merger. Not unlike a typical teenager throwing a tantrum when she panics, I screamed, slammed doors, and repeatedly vowed, "I'm not going."

With time, however, a whisper in my soul said, "It's your time now, Heidi, to shine!"

That summer, I bought new clothes, styled my hair differently, watched myself in the mirror, and practiced smiling and having engaging conversations. I diligently practiced everything I observed the popular girls doing. I acted *as if* I was confident. I wanted to leave that shy girl behind.

And you know what? It worked! I walked into my new school and all the girls wanted to be my friend. All the boys wanted to go steady. I enjoyed the attention. There was still the shy girl within me, yet I allowed myself to play a different part.

In the mid-1980s, I moved to Los Angeles to earn my master's degree in psychology at Pepperdine University. Living in the big city, and not knowing anyone, brought the return of that shy little girl. I was working as a therapist and was within my comfort zone working one-on-one with my clients.

I was then introduced to my very first women's networking organization to make new connections. I was overwhelmed with the excitement of these powerful entrepreneurial women. I experienced and observed them conducting business with one another and watched them speak at the podium with such enthusiasm and magnificent energy. *Wow*, I thought, *I want to be like these women.*

However, at the time, I would retreat to the ladies' room and wait for the meeting to start. Then I'd slowly and quietly find my seat. I didn't know how to network and felt I had nothing to say. My shy self took over. Yet, I longed to be out there mixing and mingling with these empowering women.

I kept returning to these meetings. Many of these women were offering various personal and professional development classes, such as: How To Be More Confident, How To Be A Public

Speaker, How To Dress For Success, Acting Classes For Non-Actors, and on it went.

I took advantage of everything. I started investing in *me*. On my journey of self-discovery, something wondrous slowly, very slowly, began to happen.

I began to believe in myself. I wanted to be able to speak out and be heard with confidence. I knew it was time for me to make a difference and hopefully an impact.

It was not long after that I found the courage to open my own consulting business, combining my therapeutic training with my love of acting. The gift of being able to empower women to find their inner and outer voice; to communicate who they are; to build stronger relationships both personally and professionally; to be able to shine and trust they are beautiful; and to give them permission to go for their dreams, to follow their heart; to find their true purpose for being here on this planet; and to enable other women to recognize their gifts became my gift, my passion, and my mission.

After attending my 25th McDowell High School class reunion in 2003—and meeting the man (Phil Kerner) I was destined to marry—I returned to Erie the following year, newly married, and resumed my career as a motivational speaker.

Unable to find a similar type of networking as I had experienced previously, I took it upon myself and created the Coffee Club Divas, a group of more than 100 women coming together virtually from all over the world once a month to connect, support one another personally and professionally, learn to become comfortable with themselves, find out how to stand up and be heard. and at the same time, have fun as they release their inner diva and allow her to shine!

Ironically, the demographics within this group include women as young as their early 20s to women in their 50s, 60s, and 70s. They are saying *yes* to their time to shine. They are unwrapping their gifts, recreating their businesses, and making an impact.

My wish for you and women like Carol is to believe that it's not too late. This is a wonderful time of life to share the precious gift of you and let your inner light SHINE!

## About Heidi

Heidi Parr Kerner is the founder and creator of The Coffee Club Divas, a women's networking organization. She provides step-by-step guidance to assist others out of their comfort zone to live boldly and confidently in their business and personal lives.

Heidi has positioned herself as a leader in the arena of women's empowerment, business networking, motivational speaking, sales training, and transformational change.

With a master's degree in psychology, her coast-to-coast career spans over 25 years and includes roles as a certified career coach, workshop facilitator, radio host, actress, producer, author, and keynote speaker.

She was the recipient of the prestigious Women Making History award in 2019.

Her clients include Fortune 500 and 100 companies, small businesses, nonprofits, universities, hospitals, and professional associations. As a seasoned business owner and marketing consultant, she is especially passionate about mentoring women entrepreneurs and professionals.

On a personal note, Heidi is very involved in community theater, the arts, dancing, and performing locally. She also loves to travel with her husband, Phil.

**Connect with Heidi**

heidi@heidiinspired.com

www.heidiinspired.com

www.coffeeclubdivas.com

# Let Your Story Find You and in It You Will Find Yourself

**Theresa Ream**

"The weakest part of your life can become the strongest part of your story."

- Sean Abbananto

Dear Seeker,

There is a great power that lies within our stories. Some of our stories will be deeply influenced by our mothers, grandmothers, and people who either enriched our lives or were destructive influences. When we neglect to get in touch with our stories, we go through our lives not totally understanding the place called our *soul home*. Some stories go untold, and some are never made known to even us. When we don't know our story, we are not rooted and can easily be blown here and there by the opinions of others. I believe this is mostly true for us women. Our instincts are cut away, we are taught to behave and not be ourselves. We are rendered diluted somehow through a stifling domestication that causes us to lose self-protection against predators and vampires in regular peoples' clothing.

Knowing our own stories allows us to take hold of following our dreams. Sometimes we will be seen as outsiders for pursuing our dreams. In our pursuit, we may be filled with powerful thoughts and ideas that don't fit the box the world has put us in; but what is the impact on our souls if we continue to spend years with those that don't support what is true and good for us?

So dear one, let me tell you a small part of my story in the hopes that you will realize your story is powerful too and can be the platform on which you orchestrate your life.

**Against All Odds**

I am the proud owner of a multimillion dollar, multigenerational, minority, woman-owned business. My life was very much influenced by my mother Juanita Louisa Santos. I wouldn't be who I am without the influence of her story. She had a fantastic history: she grew up in very tragic circumstances but against all odds, my mother became the first minority businesswoman in the small town that I grew up in.

From an early age, it was ingrained in me that women are very strong and can do anything they put their minds to. She had a very keen instinctual nature and taught me how to read people and animals and about the sacredness of nurturing life. Maybe her story made her the way she was and brought her strength when it could have just as easily made her a victim. She was a survivor of extremely abusive alcoholic parents. They were migrant field workers of the 1920s and 1930s. She grew up living in tents and cars along the fertile valleys of California. Life was terrifying as her parents ravaged her world with violence. She was sad on her birthdays because her mother told her she tried to get rid of her by putting a coat hanger into her womb. My grandmother told my mother, "You fought hard through all the blood, and you still lived."

My mother persevered and went on to graduate high school with honors at the age of fifteen. She was so beautiful that she also earned her way through school, working as a model for a local artist.

She married at 17 years old, gave birth to her first child at 18, and started a business with literally no money. My mother worked hard not only in the business but physically constructing the buildings in which her businesses were housed.

We struggled as she put my older brother through college; he literally became a rocket scientist working for General Dynamics. Those years were extra lean. My childhood was good in many ways but the darkness of not being accepted socially really hit a painful cord that I still struggle with today. My younger self had to live through times of poverty, times of ugly dirty hand me downs, and homes that were to most people considered shacks. Eventually, we started to do better financially and even got a new house, but the pain of non-acceptance carried over into my adult life. It took me many decades to work through thinking I was not good enough in some way and still I find myself worrying about being judged. I think it was good, as it made me try harder to be better. I believe for many women non-acceptance by others can carry over to non-acceptance of self.

**Your Childhood Dreams Can Leave Clues**

Our lives are woven with so many textures and colors that I have always known if my life had a name, it would be Serendipity. The opportunities that came to and through my life are full of random happenings that are both good and bad.

As I grew older, the dreams of being someone who would be able to make a difference to those around me strengthened. I noticed a man in our community who was deemed a hero by the locals. He was a restoration contractor who I witnessed showing up to homes that had fires, consoling people on their porches, telling them that everything was going to be all right. He would then rebuild their homes, and everyone was happy. I thought of someday being like him. I think it's important to listen to our childhood dreams because so many of us get tied into the grown-up dreams of someone else. Go back and start cultivating your childhood hopes and dreams and see what grows.

At 16, I decided to write out a vision for my perfect husband, down to his personality and the color of his eyes and hair. Six months later, as fate would have it, I met him in a super-random way. I was set up on a blind date that evening with a rather unappealing guy. As we walked into a restaurant, the vision of my dream husband in the flesh walked out. Alas, my blind date was friends with my future husband's roommate. We dated for six years and were married when I turned 22 years old.

## Sometimes We Don't Recognize Our Dreams Taking Form in the Beginning

In our third year of marriage, we opened our first business. We always loved houses, so my husband earned his building contractor's license, and we started our journey as business owners. Being in business does not always look like you dreamed it to be. That's why many businesses fail in the first five years. It's hard; you can't afford to pay yourself and what you do daily doesn't look in the slightest like what you envisioned.

During the first five years, I worked as a waitress by day and a hairdresser by night. We even took on a partner for five years. At the five-year mark, we were making enough from the business to support us, and we bought the partner out; I had my first child and started to work full-time in the company. Being the owner

27

doesn't always mean you start at the top. I started at the very bottom as the person that takes debris to the dump, cleans up job sites and does demo work. I was totally horrible at it. One day, I thought, *this isn't helping the business,* and I went back to college. I took courses to learn business law and accounting, so I wouldn't have to work in the field.

If you are thinking of going into business, note that the number one thing that business owners do backward is put production in charge of accounting. I am going to let you in on a business secret—administration must control the money and take control of production if they go out of systems. I believe businesses fail because of this backward way of thinking. Setting up the accounting and administration team to take control of my company was a hard decision. It didn't go over well with production and over a decade later it still doesn't at times. Making decisions can be scary. We all must make hard choices and the people closest to us can be unsupportive and at times sabotaging. Sometimes we just need to be strong enough to let the people we care about be disappointed in our decisions. It may be time to look at our fears about our own truths. Looking back, I would have done things differently. I would have started at the top as an owner. At the time, I didn't know my strengths were in administration and marketing. I would urge you to know yourself better so you can make good choices.

## A Childhood Dream Catches up with Me

As we lay sleeping one fateful night at 2 a.m., a drunk driver drove his car into our home. If someone had told me that the course of my life would change that night, I would not have believed them. The next day an adjuster from our insurance company came to look at the damage and asked what we did for a living. I told him we were building contractors. He asked if we did insurance work. I said, "absolutely!" Well, not yet actually, but I didn't mention that. That week we bid our first insurance work and so my dream began.

## "Yes" Is a Beautiful Word

The business grew, but not because we planned it. I felt a pang of shame as I wrote the last sentence. Aren't all good businesswomen supposed to plan? Planning didn't grow the large company I had dreamed of owning. It was serendipity that started the ball rolling. One by one people with experience came to us and asked us to open more divisions, and we said *yes*. You know, yes, it is a beautiful place to live. There is a freedom in yes, the *yes* that almost doesn't care if we fail because we know we can get back up and do it again. Soon, not only did I have a construction division but a fire and water mitigation division, an environmental cleanup division, and two retail stores consisting of a flooring store and a high-end cabinet store. All because people that wanted to work for us asked if they could start those divisions, and we said *yes*. The values statement of our company is "Grow the individual, build the family, inspire the community and enrich the world." That is our truth. We took chances on people—some didn't work out and some were rock stars—but it all worked toward a greater good, for both my business and the people we took a chance on. As I write this, I think of all the women that didn't say *yes*. Without saying *yes* and taking risks, our worlds can become small. I don't think dreams can come true without a *yes*.

**Relationships Are Highly Undervalued**

Would our lives be better if we had taken more time to nurture past relationships that tumbled, fell into, or roared through our lives? How would our lives be different with the support that could have been? How many life-changing relationships did we let slip away? Too busy, not enough energy, not enough time, poor communication—whatever the excuse—what have we lost? I truly believe the quality of our relationships equals the quality of our lives.

Dear one, don't put the nurturing of current relationships or the energy it takes to create new relationships on the back burner. I love the saying: *you never know where and when you will meet the person that changes your life forever!*

In closing our heartfelt talk, I leave you with this: the biggest adversity to overcome is to know yourself. It took years to swim the mote of well-meaning opinions to get to the castle named *soul house.* To know yourself takes a great deal of time spent walking a hot dusty road with stones hurled at your soul from the sidelines. Sometimes the stones are thrown in the name of love. So, dear one, please pick up the stones because they will build your castle.

## About Theresa

Theresa Ream is the founder of several multimillion-dollar businesses known as the Ream Companies and has over 40 years of success. She is known as the largest minority woman-owned restoration company on the central coast and beyond. The Ream Companies consist of Disaster Kleenup Specialists, Flooring America's Floor Store USA, and Cypress Build and Cabinet Design.

Theresa is a two-time recipient of KSBW-TV/Union Bank's Best Woman Owned Business and Best Minority Owned business along with being named The Woman of the Year by The Professional Women's Network of Monterey.

Theresa has served on numerous boards. She is a people connector, and her passion is helping women entrepreneurs. She utilizes her strong organizational, financial, and marketing skills to mentor and nurture women growing them and their businesses thru coaching them in systems, marketing, and mastering their networking skills

Theresa is a community leader, speaker, author, blogger, a quarterly expert business writer for Marketing, Media and Money Magazine, podcast guest, cohost of PWN's *Ask The Expert* show, as well as the current president of the Professional Women's Network of the Monterey Peninsula.

When Theresa is not serving in her business and community, she is an avid reader and traveler, loves boot camp, riding her bike, and happily raising and homeschooling her ten-year-old grandson Cash with her husband Terry.

**Connect with Theresa**

theresa@reamteam77.com

https://www.facebook.com/theresa.ream.98

https://www.linkedin.com/in/theresaream

# How to Get to Paris Like a Pro!

## My Path to Alcohol Freedom

### Jody Royee

"Calmness of mind is one of the beautiful jewels of wisdom. It is the result of long and patient effort in self-control. Its presence is an indication of ripened experience, and of a more than ordinary knowledge of the laws and operations of thought."[2]

- James Allen

I hate clowns, and I hate those creepy china dolls that sit stone cold on the shelves of little girls' bedrooms staring blankly into space, frozen in time and waiting to come alive. It's like they are

---

[2] Allen, James. Calmness Of Mind - The Economic Times (indiatimes.com)

under a hypnotic spell, just waiting to be released from their captor's trance.

God, look where my mind goes! Maybe that's why I was attracted to horror movies as a child? Maybe I'm trying to get past the demons by facing them head-on? Why should I be so triggered by clowns and inanimate harmless china dolls? Why does my mind assign them the role of *the evildoer*? Why get so emotionally involved in ridiculous thoughts? It's all in my imagination, right?

This imagination thing can be like a sucking black hole of impending doom. It's like a blessing and a curse. It's like being trapped in a deep pit with no lifeline back to the surface where the sun is shining. It's like an astronaut untethered, floating aimlessly in the blackness of space just waiting for the oxygen to run out.

Clearly, that's why I drink! My mind is a 12-lane highway running senseless activity back and forth with a huge chance for an accident. Facing these imaginations seems to just make them more dramatic. As if I'm purposely walking into a horror movie to face my fears only to find I'm a captive audience, and I paid for it. The story gets darker, and just when you think it can't get any worse, it does. The imagination offers up yet another scenario, more evil than the last.

Hell with this! Let's tune out the noise and have a glass of wine.

I'll tell you what I do love: God, my friends and family, Paris in the summer, flying first class, and waking up in luxury accommodations with a beautiful sun rising on the water. For my 60th birthday, I decided to celebrate with my partner and two closest friends. We were going to Paris to enjoy a 5-star river boat cruise on the Seine River. This was going to be a trip I'd remember for the rest of my life.

The gate agent called our 7:30 p.m. British Air flight to London. I wasn't happy about our six-hour layover, but Paris was waiting. I reached for the body wallet around my neck, and it was gone, along with my passport and 800 euros. Immediate panic set in.

I got through security, maybe it was back there? I rummaged through my carry-ons with no luck. Announcing my dilemma to the group, I left them to search my bags and sprinted off to retrace every spot we had visited in the three hours of revelry we'd spent before boarding. The path through the terminal began at security which led to the California Wine Bar, multiple shopping opportunities, a sake bar, and finally our gate. I found no wallet and I was without a passport to travel, never mind the 800 euro. I jetted back to the gate at the end of the terminal just in time to see that everyone, but my friends, had boarded. The carry-ons were neatly assembled off to the side.

To my horror, the friendly gate agent greeted me with, "Ma'am we are pulling your bags off the plane. You will have to get a new passport and join your friends on another flight."

No! This cannot be happening! I was a former international travel agent. I had been to 26 countries and never missed any of my flights.

I refused my friends' offers to stay and help me, just as the gate agent quickly agreed, "Let her figure this out on her own, she will be fine."

*Gee, thanks lady!* But little did I know, this was the voice of God!

I sadly hugged everyone and waved goodbye with tears in my eyes, my partner and two friends left my view. I stood at the window and watched as the plane rolled back and headed for the runway. I was in a nightmare that I could not wake up from. What the hell was I going to do on a Friday night to get myself to Paris in time to board that riverboat?

First, I had to find a seat, calm down, and sober up. After two glasses of wine and a bottle of sake, I realized I was the cause of my own dilemma. I needed to hear *the voice*—He, She, It, God, Jesus, Holy Spirit, the Universe—always talked to me when I tuned in. Now, I was getting a big fat zero on the radar screen. Was it the alcohol?

*Hello! Yes, you idiot!* That voice was loud and clear.

My soul was crying out, *please, please, please tell me where my passport is?* That's all I really cared about because I knew I couldn't get an emergency passport until Monday, and I'd have to go to San Francisco. I needed to find it or create a strategy to get a new one. I needed to know what to do, and my mind was racing. I had to calm down. My Spidey senses were not working.

I've heard *the voice* my whole life, but I don't always listen.

Am I supposed to spend the night in San Jose? Go to San Francisco? I'll need a new airline ticket to replace the non-refundable one I just lost because I was recorded as a *no-show*. The financial losses are starting to add up in my mind. *Shut up! I need to hear from God, not my inner accountant!*

I'm sitting alone at 8 p.m. in a San Jose, Ca. airport terminal arguing with myself.

Welcome to your 60s Jody.

Now the inner critic has new ammunition to shoot at me. Oh no, this is not going well. Meanwhile, my bags are downstairs, and I am not going to miss picking them up.

So, let's get going sister, you'll figure out something along the way.

Jumping on the escalator down to baggage claim I heard the voice: Go get a rental car and drive home. You'll be back tomorrow.

Wait, What? Tomorrow? How?

Just do it!

I was all sobered up by now. With my bags in the trunk of my rental car, I headed home to Monterey. The cat sitter would be shocked if I just drove up, so I alerted her to my situation. Now, it was time for a mindset shift and an attitude adjustment; *the voice* is finally coming through. It was time for songs of praise and gratitude, all the way home. I had to stir up my faith and get my heart and mind in the right place.

During times of struggle, I'm so grateful I have songs and words of wisdom deeply planted into my mental storehouse because after all the monkey-mind chatter dies down, the wisdom floats to the surface and reminds me of whose I am and what is true.

I'll share just one of my favorite bible verses:

"Trust in the LORD with all your heart, And lean not on your own understanding; In all your ways acknowledge Him, And He shall direct your paths."[3] (Pro 3:5-6)

As I pulled my luggage through the doorway of my kitchen and stood in the narrow short hallway staring at the white two-door refrigerator, I asked one more time, *where is my passport?*

Look down and put your hand into the void where your carry-on handles press in.

As fast as lightning I plunged my hand into the black cavity and felt the fake leather wallet in my hand. Are you serious? I had it the entire time!

Well, I'm clearly the problem in this little melodrama called Jody's life. *Ok, now what? Oh, and by the way, thank you!*

Cancel your return flight, book a new set of tickets, and call your friends!

Yes sir!

I lost the cost of my round-trip ticket making this an expensive lesson. I had no idea what was facing me for a next-day flight to Paris, so I was ready for a shock.

---

[3] Pro 3:5-6 (NKJV)

Google revealed a result I never expected: XL Airways was going nonstop from San Francisco to Paris. They quoted $267.00 one way. *No way!* Is this one of those internet scams? My eyes didn't believe what I was seeing. Tomorrow's flight was leaving at 3:30 p.m. and arriving at 11:30 a.m. the next day. This means I would arrive in time for our first excursion in Paris, a trip up to the top of the Eiffel Tower.

My friends were headed toward that nasty six-hour Heathrow layover. Their next flight got them to Paris at 10 p.m. the next day. This is like a time-travel miracle. I get to sleep in my own bed and arrive the same day we start our Paris fun. I called Karen and left her a message! It's hard to believe that I'm back in the game. And this is where the real story begins ... but it wasn't until I returned from our wonderful time in France. We were drinking wine every day, eating amazing food, and soaking in the beauty of the Seine countryside from Paris to Étretat. The whole time on the ship I knew there was an Alcoholics Anonymous (AA) meeting every day. But it was my birthday celebration, so I was not giving up alcohol this time around. Yea, I'd been to AA since I was 21 years old, quitting on and off for years. If I did this again it would be number four.

I knew I was powerless over alcohol. I knew the 12 Steps and had walked them many times. I knew alcohol was a toxic poison. I knew it ruined my life, but God was on my side and things always seemed to work out so why quit now?

*Just don't get drunk and lose your wallet and passport Jody! OK?*
That *voice* was still talking too; I was still a prisoner of the demon.
I was going home soon, so I better make a plan.

A few weeks after getting home I walked into a local AA
women's only meeting with my sober girlfriend. On the wall was
a huge poster of the 12 Steps. I just stood there, transfixed, and
focused on reading slowly down the list.

In absolute shock, I saw two steps that my mind had not
processed before now. How did I miss those?

"6. We're entirely ready to have God remove all these defects
of character."

"7. Humbly asked Him to remove our shortcomings."

There they were, smack in the middle, the power center of the
whole deliverance-package.

I got to Step 12.

"12. Having had a spiritual awakening as the result of these
steps, we carry this message to other alcoholics and practice these
principles in all our affairs."

Boom!

Literally, it was like I got a reboot—a new hard-drive and new software to operate from. God delivered me from me.

The old me is an alcoholic for sure but that day she died, September 10, 2019. I could resurrect her if I wanted to—I have that power and the choice to do so—but I get to live as this new person who is sober and free. I get to continue to practice being this new me and grow into the person I'm meant to become.

Maybe you need a spiritual reboot, so I leave you with this:

- Ask for what you think is not available for you and be persistent.
- The impossible is possible with *the voice of God.*

## About Jody

Jody grew up in Los Angeles, Ca. She learned to swim at three years old, ski at five, and sailboat at eight. She played every sport she could and started traveling the world with her family at 13 years old. Jody is fearless and adventurous.

One of her many gifts, besides digital art photography and design, is helping people tune inside and become aware of their divine inner voice of guidance.

As a certified hypnotherapist, Jody helps people actualize their hidden dreams and abandoned desires.

Jody helps people find their inner peace and master the power of their minds so they can confidently and consistently move in the direction of their spiritual vision. She also helps people navigate the scary transitions and unfamiliar territory that following their path requires. She helps people break through the terror barriers that hold them captive in fear, anxiety, lack, and limiting paradigms.

Jody is a first-generation Polish American on her dad's side and her mom's family immigrated from France in the 1600s. After graduating from USC Fine Art School in photography and sculpture, Jody taught art in Los Angeles for eight years. She traded her teaching career for world travel and traded her darkroom for a digital camera and the biggest iMac on the market. Jody is grateful to have traveled to 26 countries and island nations. The influence of other cultures is vital to her embrace of the unfamiliar, her level of gratitude, and her joyful nature.

Jody moved from Los Angeles to the Monterey Peninsula in 1990 and lives in beautiful Carmel Valley. She is grateful every day for her relationship with Jesus, her life partner Karen, and her family and friends. She enjoys being with her animals, hiking and biking in nature, and traveling the world.

With God All Things Are Possible.

**Connect with Jody**

www.jodyroyee.com

montereymarketing360@gmail.com

# A Mother's Journey Finding Peace, Success, and Purpose

**Tammy S. Ward**

"That which does not kill us makes us stronger."[4]

- Friedrich Nietzsche

The first time I saw this quote it spoke to me. I had overcome, survived, even thrived. I didn't know how much it would continue to be a theme in my life.

I grew up with this on the wall in our home, "God grant me the Serenity to accept the things I cannot change, the Courage to change the things I can, and the WISDOM to know the

---

[4] Nietzsche, Friedrich. *Twilight of the Idols*, Maxims and Arrows, 1889, https://www.oxfordreference.com/view/10.1093/acref/9780191843730.001.0001/q-oro-ed5-00007886

difference." Great words to live by; however, not always easy to implement. I referred to this often, but little did I know its true significance. God was equipping me for the most difficult and heartbreaking chapter of my life.

I was blessed to grow up in a household with nurturing and supportive parents. They taught us to believe in the power of our attitudes and thoughts. I had a stay-at-home mom and an entrepreneurial dad. Together they were the perfect balance. They taught us to smile, to think for ourselves, and to look for the silver lining because there *always* is one. We are a tight-knit family. I have two sisters and a brother, and these amazing siblings are my best friends! I know this gave me my edge in life. I am grateful for their love and support—yet another way God was equipping me.

As a single mother raising two sons, Bryan and Trevor, we were very close. It was the three of us against the world. So, when I met a wonderful man who adored us and married him in 2006, it was an adjustment—albeit a good one.

Happily married with my oldest in the military and my youngest heading off to college, I was entering the *empty nest* stage of life. I had some trepidations, especially regarding Trevor. Originally, I chalked it up to senioritis but even during the summer something seemed amiss. He assured me he was fine, just all the changes. Never ignore your mother's instincts!

This time was a transition for us all. I love being a mom, always will, and I missed my boys. However, it was also a time to reflect, redirect, and figure out what I wanted to do with the rest of my life. The possibilities were endless! Audrey Hepburn said, "Nothing is impossible, the word itself says, 'I'm possible!'"[5] It was both exhilarating and scary. Change is like that. I chose to embrace the excitement and let go of fear because I knew I wanted to grow and find my new purpose.

I could hear my dad, the supreme optimist, saying, "Attitude is everything, Tammy Sue. It will make or break you." I chose to have a positive one, and it is a choice. We can't control what happens to us, but we can choose how we react; and therefore, how it affects us. It's one of the few things we can control. I was about to learn that all too well!

Trevor was struggling. He'd been an A student but was failing and missing classes. We'd always been close and communicated well, so when he assured me, he was just adjusting to being on his own and had it under control, we let him go back to school to give it another try. I felt he deserved the chance. I knew him and what he was capable of, but the nagging feeling remained. He improved his first month back; however, the decline started again.

---

[5] Hepburn, Audrey, Audrey Hepburn Best Quotes | British Vogue | British Vogue

I knew something was wrong. I called him on a Saturday in March and said, "Trevor, I love you with all my heart, and I know something is wrong. You're not OK." Never in a million years did I expect his response, "Mom, you're right. I'm not. I'm doing drugs. I'm a heroin addict."

Thank God I was sitting down, or I would've collapsed to the floor. I'd been struck hard. My heart sank to a depth I didn't know existed. It was pounding frantically and yet broken at the same time. My eyes welled up, my baby's a heroin addict.

I calmly asked, "how long?"

"A while."

"Pills or IV?"

"Pills."

I thought, thank God he didn't cross that line. You already know I'm a glass half-full, silver-lining-type person. I believed IV use would make it even harder to break the addiction, and at least that was in our favor. I responded, "OK, we're going to beat this sweetie." Thankfully, I've always been good in a crisis and able to do whatever needs to be done in the moment, dealing with the rest later.

Without skipping a beat, I said, "Start packing because I'll be in the car in the next ten minutes to bring you home. I love you."

"Alright. I love you too, Mom."

I wish I could say that was the end. He went into intense outpatient treatment (IOP) and once completed, he was fine but that isn't any addict's story. Relapse is part of recovery.

He went out one night, and it was a week before he returned. I was heartbroken, panicked, and prayed constantly. The night he came knocking on the door, God had given me the strength of Atlas in advance of my needing it. I had arisen in the morning feeling different, I just didn't know why at the time.

I answered the door to him standing on the threshold with me just inside. I told him I wouldn't help him kill himself, nor watch because I loved him too much. He could come home if he'd go into rehab. He looked up occasionally and then back down. He hemmed and hawed for what seemed like a lifetime. Finally, he looked up with sad, teary, soulful eyes and said, "Mom, I can't." So, we packed him up and dropped him and his duffel bag off at a friend's house. I said, I "love you with all my heart and am always here for you whenever you want, need, or are ready." He said he loved me too, and we hugged. There is no doubt there was only one set of *footprints*[6] in the sand that day.

---

[6] Footprints in the Sand, "Footprints in the Sand" Poem Meaning & Biblical Hope (crosswalk.com)

I was doing my best, trying to stay in the moment, live my life, and function. However, it was always there weighing on my mind, heart, and soul. The fear, worry, questions, doubts—wanting to fix it and knowing I couldn't—feeling helpless yet grasping tightly to hope. He was alive and that was my silver lining for now. I was sure this was hell, and if I wasn't careful, it could consume me.

I knew I needed a focus—a positive distraction—to be of service to others, to be around uplifting people, and to experience some fun. I wasn't going to become lost in his addiction. I needed flexibility and extra income to help towards his rehab, as well as a phone—his lifeline and my sanity. I investigated a network marketing company whose products I loved, and priorities matched mine. In August 2008, I joined Mary Kay cosmetics and started my entrepreneurial journey.

I wish I could say it was smooth sailing; however, anything new we do involves growing pains and work. I've heard it said, *Network marketing is personal growth disguised as a business.* This is so true! Where there is growth there is fruit. To be successful in life or business, we must grow. It's the greatest gift that came from my business. I've blossomed in so many ways, and it was a lifesaver for me.

I love to learn, it's fun! However, the implementation was a whole other beast.

I'm what you call an extroverted introvert. I'm a homebody who socializes well but needs quiet time to refill my cup. Having a small circle of friends, I needed to step out of my comfort zone and talk to strangers. I decided I'd talk to three women while grocery shopping. Everything starts with a decision. An hour later, after chickening out each time, I headed for the door. With each step, the disappointment in myself increased. I'm not a quitter! I went and approached three ladies. I didn't get a booking, but I did it. Success!

I realized, being a giver by nature, I felt like I was asking for a favor. I remember my national sales director asking me, "Did you enjoy your facial and makeover when you were offered one?" "Yes!" I responded. "Change your thinking. You're offering, not asking. You're giving her a gift," she explained to me. Wow—a light went off.

Still, limiting beliefs and stumbling blocks cropped up—the fear of failure surprised me. I thought I was courageous, a fearless warrior! Look at all I had and was facing. I persevered, and my business and I continued to grow. Yet, underneath it all was the heartbreak of my son's life being in jeopardy. I learned everything I could about addiction because knowledge is power. There was always a litany of prayers running through my head except when I was pampering a woman: helping enhance her natural beauty, boosting her overall confidence, and making her feel special. There was relief through serving and leaning on the Lord.

In 2012, I earned the use of my first car. The timing was perfect because it allowed me to visit my son who just entered rehab. I am happy to say he's ten years clean and sober!

I earned the use of three more cars, was number one in sales in our national area, and built a successful business. Then the pandemic hit, and my face-to-face business came to a halt. I had to decide whether to pivot or just maintain. I pivoted. I reinvented my business by learning social media and attraction marketing. I believed I could, so I did. As Henry Ford said, "Whether you think you can, or think you can't, you're right."[7]

During that time, I soul searched. I felt strongly I had a deeper purpose. So, I asked God and he showed me speaking to a group of women. *Are you sure, God?* The next day he showed me again. *OK, but I need more clarity, this could be anything.* The following day he showed me speaking to the crowd with Trevor at my side. This was powerful! I was to help moms with children in addiction.

Teachers learn the concepts they're teaching from a course, whereas mentors carry breakthrough and authority because they've gone through what they're teaching. I've created a

---

[7] Ford, Henry, www.forbes.com 21 quotes from Hendry Ford on business, leadership and life by Erika Andersen May 31, 2013

program, Unbound Love: Mentoring Moms with Children in Addiction.

I want to help parents live while their child is lost; to have peace regardless of the choices their child makes or the outcome. I'll share the tools it took me years to garner, thereby shortening their learning curve, as addiction doesn't come with a handbook.

God gave me the strength and guidance to get out of the pit and be the beacon my son needed to guide him home. I help moms embrace their own recovery, break the bondage, and navigate the difficulties of this journey. They will become a beacon of love, light, and hope, standing strong and able to help when their child's ready for a better life. They will experience a new unbound love for their child and themselves, and they will know the boundless love God has for them both.

I'm in the process of being certified as a life coach. I'll use and share these navigation tools to bring even greater transformation and breakthrough because as I said, addiction doesn't come with a handbook.

I didn't know this is where my journey would lead, or what this next chapter will bring. I do know God turns all things to good. "Trust in the Lord with all your heart and do not lean on your own understanding. In all your ways acknowledge him, and he will make straight your paths."[8] (Pr 3:5-6) My story isn't over because instead of stopping I turned the page.

What are your struggles, hopes, and dreams? What's holding you back? Know that you too are an overcomer. Find a way to turn the page, embrace the next chapter, and ignite your passion and purpose. You'll bless many including yourself.

**About Tammy**

**Photo by Acacia Studios**

Tammy S. Ward is an entrepreneur running her businesses with kingdom principles.

---

[8] Pr 3:5-6 (ESV)

She is the creator of Unbound Love: Mentoring Moms with Children in Addiction. Having gained knowledge, skills, and experience through her own struggles, she wants to empower other moms. It is now her passion to help moms learn to live while their child is lost, find peace, and provide the necessary tools to navigate this difficult journey.

She also created Beauty and Beyond: Beauty of Mind, Body, and Spirit–glow from the inside out. As an independent Mary Kay beauty consultant for over 13 years, she has helped women bring their inner beauty out by enhancing their natural beauty and boosting overall confidence. It is her joy to help and be of service to others.

**Connect with Tammy**

www.facebook.com/tammy.ward.988

www.unboundlovementoring.com

tammywardmk@gmail.com

20 Lives Ignited

# Blazing New Trails

## Women Forging Paths

# Now I Know

## Gae Anderson Miller

"Sometimes, you have to get hit in the face with a baseball bat a couple of times before you realize how good you look with your teeth capped!"

James A. West

I bet you're thinking, *why would this gal start a story in such a graphic way?* Well, I need to share that when something bad happens to you, it is important to acknowledge what the hurt from setbacks feels like, so you can embrace it, accept it, and truly move on. The quote above came in a hand-drawn card sent to me by a friend when I was at rock bottom. It depicts the reality of my first baseball bat experience and how it helped me grow.

At the end of my 12th year of public-school teaching (a long time ago), I was asked by directors at a private school if I would accept the position as the first female head of their independent K-8 school. I couldn't wrap my head around the idea because I was happy and successful at what I was doing. My gut said, *why should I make a change?* To drop my perfect job and take such a giant leap into the unknown was scary.

My teacher evaluations in the school district were stellar. I wrote a few computer handbooks for teachers and a book for parents of gifted children. My students excelled in academics and problem-solving competitions, and I developed a great rapport with their parents. However, I started getting teacher evaluations that said I was, "too enthusiastic" and that I "shouldn't be any better than any members of my team."

Feeling hurt that my efforts, ambition, and dedication weren't recognized, I thought, *Dang! Why not?* So, I said goodbye to my students and teacher friends and dug my heels in for this new adventure as the administrative head of the school with the promise of the full support of the board.

When I moved into my new office, I discovered that the school was in financial trouble, enrollment was down, and the rigor of the school needed bolstering. I was directed to take immediate action to improve the course of the school to keep it open. Tenaciously working to make change, I started many programs to improve the academic and financial status of the school and created a parent welcome center filled with resources.

Things were going quite smoothly. I connected with the parents, and I felt productive while spending 12-14 hours a day at work. However, I learned about special arrangements that I was expected to make. Without getting into detail, I discovered that I was to bend the rules for the children of the parents who were financially backing the school. I did not believe that was a fair thing to do.

Soon after that, I was asked to attend a board meeting at a law firm in town, away from the school setting. Excited, I saw this as an opportunity to share the improved parent relations and academic success of the school. So, I created a media presentation and was prepared to share it with the board at the meeting. I was completely unaware of the baseball bat that was headed my way.

When I entered the conference room of a large law firm, the smell of leather chairs and law books reflected the seriousness of the room. As I walked into the meeting, a shiny 20-foot solid mahogany table stared me in the face. The men of the board were already seated, and they warned me with their eyes that something terrible was about to happen.

I was abruptly denied the opportunity to share my presentation, and I suddenly felt like Daniel in the lion's den. Then, I was accused of misconduct way beyond anything I could've ever imagined. I was requested to step down from my position. I was numb from the blow of the baseball bat. Up until then, nothing about my integrity, honesty, or ethics was ever in question regarding my career. I was naïve to the fact that powerful men can do or say anything they want.

How could this happen? My mind was racing. This was the first big leap in my career, and I wanted to run back to my safe classroom and loving kids. However, I had cut the cord from being a public-school teacher.

I prayed for help. Holding back a flood of tears, the issue became a "he-said she-said" situation. With perfect posture and in a clear voice, I denounced the accusations and presented documents that proved I was right. When they refused to see them, I realized I needed to cut my losses and move on. I agreed to part ways rather than continue in a no-win situation at the school. The board knew I had strong parental supporters, so I was directed to announce that it was my decision to leave the school.

I stayed for the rest of the year while remaining professional, composed, and positive. I even directed a fundraiser at the end of the school year. Come summer, I packed my stuff and moved quietly from the building.

I still hurt from the blow of that baseball bat and couldn't seem to get my act together. Crying, searching for meaning, I tried to figure out what to do next. I was miserably stuck, while everyone I knew was happily working in their respective careers.

When I couldn't bring myself to shower, I just washed my face. I could not get out of my rut. I found Joyce Meyer sermons were helpful and forced myself to watch comedies like *I love Lucy* and *Tootsie*, which helped me remember how to laugh again. I suddenly realized that the world would not end. After crying so much, making myself laugh was a big help, and it became a little bit easier to breathe and feel human again. I started to focus on what *I* really wanted to do with my life.

With a master's degree and principal certificate in hand, I remembered how medicinal learning new things was for me. So, I applied for a doctoral program at a university in another city. Then, I got a call from the university department chair who accepted my application and asked if I would teach some education classes. The offer would allow me to complete coursework for a doctorate, all for free, in addition to a generous stipend. Somebody wanted me, and they felt like I had something to offer to the world. I said, "Yes!"

Things happened quickly after that. I convinced my husband to leave his dwindling business and helped him enroll at the same university. We got a little apartment not far from campus. While I was working on my dissertation, I found that a hospital near the university specialized in in vitro fertilization (IVF). I had been trying to get pregnant for *nine* years, and desperately longed for a baby. I completed three unsuccessful IVF treatments there. When I was defending my dissertation, a friend offered me a position to run a master's program in gifted education (my research and teaching passion) at a university further south in Virginia.

I decided that this offer and new professorship in another state was a sign from God, that He really wanted me to pursue my career and His priority was not for me to have a child. I applied and accepted the position and was prepared to make yet another big change.

Because my current university insurance covered most of the cost of treatments, I tried *one more time*, a fourth IVF treatment. As I was getting ready to board the plane to Virginia, to take on my new adventure, I received a call from the doctor, I. Was. Pregnant! At the ripe old age of 41, while in my brand-new job in Virginia, I gave birth to a beautiful baby girl, Leeanna!

I got my husband a job at the same university, remained at that Virginia university for 12 years, and earned the rank of full professor. I conducted research and wrote many grants that allowed me to share my studies throughout the country and the world. I conducted interactive workshops in mentoring at-risk youth, gifted and science education, creativity, and problem-solving. Sometimes, my miracle daughter, Leeanna, would travel with me. I became a NASA sub-contractor and wrote curriculum that aligned with their space missions. God opened a world to me that I never could have imagined.

Yes, there were more baseball bats, but my teeth were capped. I learned to see them coming and duck, most of the time. I faced a divorce and a vicious custody battle. I married thinking I could change him, but it turns out the only thing I could change was a diaper. My mom died a few years later, and I ended up remarried to a loving old friend. We decided to move back home, and I taught at a private university there. I changed jobs again to teach at a public university in the area, my fourth higher education experience. After a few years, I retired to care for my second husband when he became very ill. He died in 2014. Once again, I needed to redefine my mission in life.

Bouncing back was easier this time (teeth capped and all). I started my own business, Anderson Miller Consulting. I drew from my toolbox of workshop sessions over the years to book training sessions for school districts and community organizations. I found it delightful to manage my own schedule and share my research, ideas, and experiences with others. I discovered strength through adversity, not as a victim but as a resilient lady who can take a blow and get back up.

Thank you for letting me share my story with you. Looking back, it was a remarkable journey. Wherever you are in your life and career, face your setbacks and laugh after you've cried a bit. Pray for help to focus on what you really want. Realize that there will be some bad times and baseball bats may come your way, but you can and will survive to become an empowered woman and better than you ever thought you could be.

Don't be afraid to get your teeth capped. It doesn't hurt that much!

Side note: My daughter Leeanna, is now my son, Lee, but that's for another chapter!

## About Gae

Dr. Gae Anderson-Miller, president of Anderson Miller Consulting, is a motivational speaker, grant writer, and educational consultant specializing in methods that increase human potential, creativity, and communication. She helps others find hope for success rather than fear of failure and pinpoints specific tools designed to leverage the constant changes of life. Her team-building workshops are interactive, and participants are vigorously engaged as they learn how to solve problems in the workplace, at school, and at home.

Gae served two terms as chair of the creativity division of the National Association for Gifted Children. Also, the author of many articles about gifted and creative children, she won the International Hollingworth Award for her research on a national mentoring program for creative children.

As a former teacher and professor at four diverse universities, Gae has presented workshops at the local, state, and national level and internationally in the Philippines, Italy, Canada, Brazil, and the Netherlands.

Gae was awarded grants from NASA, the National Science Foundation (NSF), and government organizations to serve at-risk youth, science and education teachers and professors, nonprofit homeless, and prison re-entry programs.

She lives in Erie, Pennsylvania, and loves traveling, gardening, and doing crazy things with her four step-granddaughters. She is excited for her son, Lee, who is finishing his health psychology PhD program at Old Dominion University.

**Connect with Gae**

www.andersonmillerconsulting.com

www.linkedin.com/in/dr-gae-anderson-miller-48740817/

Facebook: Anderson Miller Consulting

# *Life is an Ever-Changing Adventure*

## Valerie Baltzer

"My mission in life is not to just survive, but to thrive; and to do it with some passion, some compassion, some humor, and some style."[9]

- Maya Angelou

I always like to start my life story by saying the first 20 and beyond years of my adult life were in other parts of the country: Colorado, California, Florida, Tennessee, and then I moved home to Pennsylvania. Every place I've lived, every move I've made, was a new adventure—a new state, a new job, a new house, new friends, and new cultures—a whole new me. Each move was a new chapter in my life, another chance to cocreate something new

---

[9] Angelou, Maya. 19 Inspirational Maya Angelou Quotes - Biography

and different. I made most of those moves alone. With no kids or significant other to ground me, I had a different perspective than most, and that fact, my friends, is a very sharp two-edged sword. Looking back, I wonder, was I running away from or toward something?

The current chapter, including me as the yoga instructor, spiritual healer and coach, Reiki master/teacher, and drum circle facilitator started when Mom and Dad moved in with me in 2010. Dad got my room because that is the room their furniture fit in. Mom got the guest room. As a family, we had been planning this for a while. We finished the attic so I would have my own bedroom. It wasn't long after they moved in that we decided to have a caretaker come a couple of days a week to help while I was at work. I was at *the best job of my life* at the time and being at work was my respite: the place where I knew what to expect next.

My brother and his family came pretty often. We spent a lot of time together that first summer. I was Mom and Dad's chauffeur, and we went out on day trips every chance we got. We celebrated Thanksgiving and Christmas, as well as between Christmas and New Year's. I came downstairs one morning and found Mom lying on the floor with a pillow under her head and a blanket. Dad was lying in her bed with his hands on his chest like you see in the movies when someone is laid out in a coffin. Why didn't they call me? I was right upstairs? I figured Dad heard Mom fall, or she called out to him, and he went in and helped as best he could. Looking back, I realize he was scared, frustrated, and didn't remember where he was or to call 911. Dad took care of mom as best he could with his Alzheimer's brain. The look on both their faces ... we called 911.

We spent a couple of days at the hospital while they ran tests to figure things out. The hospitalist came over when I was visiting and invited me to this little room. Mom had cancer in multiple locations in her body; we had decisions to make. Do we want to poke and prod her and do multiple tests or do I want to take her home with hospice and let her enjoy her time? Our family had talked about this a lot and Mom always had strong opinions about us putting her in a home. This was not a decision I was making alone. Next visit to the hospital was with my brother and my dad in the same little room. With Dad's Alzheimer's I'm not sure how much he understood, but he knew mom would want to be home and so did my brother. The hospital wanted to discharge her New Year's Eve. I practically begged the hospitalist to "at least give us New Year's Eve" which they did. That night mom got to watch as they brought the band in by helicopter with all the flashing lights for the New Year's Eve party. Her room had a view of the Life-Flight emergency helipad, and it was a busy New Year's Eve. Awe, we just let her have that one.

Hospice brought all the equipment: hospital bed, linens, etc. to get us set up. Mom was strong enough to get dressed and come out to the living room for about two weeks. During that time, her sister, my aunt Mary, flew here from Arizona to help us and be with her sister. We celebrated birthdays and anything we could think of. Every weekend my brother and his family came over and we had a party of some sort. Mom got to choose everything, after all this hospice thing was all about her. It was her party. Eventually, she wasn't strong enough to leave her room anymore. That's when we ended up squeezing Dad's recliner in so he could sit with her comfortably. He would sit and hold her hand as she slept. No wonder I never found a man who could live up to that kind of love and compassion. Mom passed on February 16th, I believe—no, I don't have the date etched in my memory nor do I remember Dad's date of death—those are end dates. I don't throw things out on their expiration dates either.

Aunt Mary stayed for a couple of weeks after mom passed. Home Instead became a permanent fixture in my home taking care of Dad and essentially me, which was a blessing. After Mom was gone, we realized quite quickly the true extent of Dad's Alzheimer's. I was an emotional wreck and somehow found this class at the Satchidananda Ashram in Buckingham, Va., a ten-day residential yoga retreat: Peaceful Weight Loss Through Yoga. My brother came to stay at the house with Dad, and Home Instead was there when we were at work. I was still working at *the best job* I ever had, but I took the time off work, let my brother stay with Dad, and I drove the nine hours to Yogaville by myself.

All the buildings had these weird-sounding Sanskrit names: the dorms, the classrooms, the dining hall, and even the house up the road where my group stayed and held class. I had taken some yoga classes here and there before this, but this lifestyle thing was all new to me. I was totally out of my element but did not have time to worry about or feel anything. The energy in that place and the panoramic views over the James River were awesome. Then one afternoon during a yoga session, I remember being on my back in savasana when one of the instructors said, "there is nothing left to do." That's when the flood gates opened and I cried for the first time since, well, I have no idea how long it had been. I'm talking tears running down my cheeks. This crying in front of strangers, allowing myself to be vulnerable, was a truly strange feeling. I dissociate when stressed, meaning I disconnect and dissociate myself from feelings, emotions, etc., so I don't have to feel pain. A self-preservation tactic that many utilize to avoid pain. So much happened in those ten days: so much evolution, so much letting go, so, so much.

I returned home and my brother went back to his family. In September, my older nephew moved in. His student teaching placement was here in town, so it worked out all the way around. He had a place to live, and Dad and I had some family support. Dad often got up in the middle of the night and wanted to go *home*. Living with an Alzheimer's person is like living with a three- or four-year-old. Many Alzheimer's patients are smart enough to get themselves up, dressed, and out the door, if they wanted to, so you always have to pay attention. Every time you hear them get up to go to the bathroom in the middle of the night, you listen to hear what they are doing and once you hear them back in bed, you relax and go back to sleep yourself.

My brother and I put Dad on the waiting list for the Soldiers and Sailors Home shortly after Mom passed. We got the call that they had a bed just days before Christmas. I asked if we could wait until after Christmas—the answer was no—they had to fill the bed in five days. If not now, Dad had to go to the end of the line and wait again. We had all talked about it for months, we, as a family, chose to admit Dad with hospice, which most people don't understand. Hospice is simply choosing not to fight the inevitable and just letting life take its course. In many ways, we had just talked about all these end-of-life decisions with my Gramma, Dad's mom, and then with Mom just a few months earlier. I remember a comment Dad made when we were talking about meds for Alzheimer's, "Why? Why prolong the agony?" We knew dad's opinion. Dad passed away in August and my life became very quiet.

One day while at a local yoga class, the instructor announced he had qualified his studio and could now do yoga teacher training. I knew what yoga had done for me after mom passed so I called and asked, "Can a 50-some-year-old fat lady be a yoga teacher?" was my first question. The reply was, "If a person in a wheelchair can be a yoga teacher, then yes, I think you can." It took a whole Pennsylvania winter, every weekend in a yurt for eight hours a day with just a wood stove for heat, but we did it. I became a certified YT200 yoga instructor in June of 2013. After that, I taught yoga at several locations and earned my meditation teacher training that fall.

My life got much simpler after *the best job of my life* ended but that's another story. I continued my studies of yoga, Reiki, mediumship, all the natural and spiritual healing modalities I could find. I got my end-of-life doula (EOLD) training partly because of my adventure with my mom and dad, and the journey I traveled with one of my best high school friends during her experience with cancer and hospice, which ended in 2018. In the fall of 2019, I became a certified drum circle facilitator, something new I totally enjoy.

Which pretty much brings us to today and living in the now. Trying my best to become the hippie, free spirit, lovechild I thought I was not allowed to be most of my life. I turned 65 years old this year, and I am starting a whole new chapter with all the adventures this official age brings. It is time to share the healing practices I have learned, time to take care of me for a while. Time to switch my online chair yoga classes that I started at the beginning of COVID-19 to a membership and share it with even more people. It's time to utilize all the unique perspectives I've gained by living in so many different places and learning so many cultures and ways of doing things in the world; time to start sharing *the world according to Valerie* in the podcast I have been visioning; and drum circles. I want to lead more drum circles. What's your next chapter?

## About Valerie

A self-proclaimed original wild child, Valerie was raised in rural Pennsylvania, the daughter of a small-town dentist. After graduating high school and spending a couple of years at a local college, she left the traditional path and spent the first 20-plus years of her adult life in other parts of the country: Colorado, California, back to Pennsylvania, Florida, and Tennessee. Valerie then returned home to Pennsylvania and lived the traditional corporate lifestyle while caring for her parents and helping them through hospice in her home and all that experience entails.

Education has always been part of Valerie's journey. This included studying in traditional academia: Edinboro State College in the 1970s and Palomar College in Southern California in the 1980s, where she earned her associate degree. In Florida, Valerie became the second female to graduate from the Motorcycle Mechanics Institute in Orlando. Another move, and subsequent broken ankle, brought her to the University of Tennessee at Martin in the 1990s and finally Gannon University in Erie, Pa., in the early 2000s.

Along with formal education, Valerie has been studying people, cultures, various philosophies, alternative healing, spiritual, and other healing modalities, as well as earning her end-of-life doula (EOLD) certificate. Valerie is a certified 200-hour yoga instructor, certified meditation instructor, certified YOGA WARRIORS instructor, and most recently became a drum circle facilitator after studying with Jim Donovan. Valerie is currently helping people stay strong and flexible, mind, body, breath, and spirit, so they can enjoy life now and into the future.

**Connect with Valerie**

Facebook: Joyous Spirit Yoga with Valerie

# One Bold Move

## Vicke Marz

"Change the way you look at things, and the things you look at change"[10]

- Wayne Dyer

I've heard it said that one bold move can change your life, and I agree. I made my first bold move at the age of 16. I was sitting in the auditorium with the rest of my high school, listening to a senior talk about his experiences as a foreign exchange student. The whole student body faded into the background as Jerry Rex talked about what it was like to travel by plane to Switzerland, how much fun he had learning a new language and having new experiences, and how the summer abroad was the best experience of his life. I felt like he was talking directly to me, and I was making my plans before he even finished his presentation.

---

[10] Dyer, Wayne. Success Secrets (drwaynedyer.com)

I was so inspired and couldn't wait to get home, appropriate paperwork tucked safely in my pocket. I chattered nonstop during dinner, barely noticing how my siblings rolled their eyes. After dinner and dishes, I carefully took the cherished papers out and handed them to my father. He looked them over while I happily explained how my life was about to change; how a plane would carry me to a faraway country where I would learn a new language, have amazing experiences, and make new forever friends. I could see it all in my mind's eye, and I was in that dreamland when I heard him say "no." He said *no*, my mother said *no*, and that was that. My dream was over before it had begun.

That night, instead of crying myself to sleep, I simply filled out the paperwork and signed my parents' names. What else would I have done? Thinking back now, it seems that somewhere in the back of my mind I should have realized I was doing the wrong thing, but I didn't. I was following my intuition, and besides, I still had to make it through a couple of different interviews, the semi-final cut, and then be interviewed by a panel to get final acceptance from the committee.

Fast forward two months: I was in math class when I got called down to the principal's office. I nervously made my way through the halls to his office, wondering what I had done to get summoned. Once I arrived, I was told that I was one of about 35 students in the country who had been chosen to participate in the

American Field Service (AFS) Summer Abroad Program for the Summer of 1979. I was on my way!

That night, I told my parents I had been accepted to the program and, of course, they forbade me to go any further. I am sure they thought they were doing the *right* thing by telling me I was on my own, and that they would not pay one penny of the expenses I was about to incur. I am sure they thought that if they told me I had to pay all of it, I would be dissuaded. They were wrong. I had a job, two actually, and I vowed to save every penny. I could, and would, do this thing on my own. I had made the decision to go, no matter what.

On June 19, 1979, I boarded a plane to Miami for a three-day orientation, then boarded another plane to Rio de Janeiro, Brazil. From Rio, I boarded a bus for a day-long trip to Rio Claro where I spent the summer. This experience forever changed me. I lived with a family who had seven other children, ages ranging from seven years old to 18 years old. My parents were amazing, my siblings were warm, friendly, funny, and crazy! I turned 17 that summer, the day before I came back to the United States. I graduated from high school in 1980 and immediately went back to Brazil to teach English, living again with the same family. I stayed there for a little less than a year and came back to the states, forever changed. For 40 and beyond years, we have remained close: visiting one another, attending weddings, funerals, and birthday parties. We talk at least once a week, sometimes more often.

That bold decision was not the last or even the most life-changing one. In 1984, I was a waitress at a local restaurant, serving breakfast and lunch Monday through Saturday. The restaurant was a family-owned place, with regular clientele coming in for lunch. One of these regulars was a man who worked at the employment office across the street. One day, he asked me if I would like to apply for a job at the local power company. Without asking a single question, I said "absolutely!" I knew I was destined for great things, and I also knew that I would need a better job if I ever wanted to have the freedom to travel back and forth to Brazil.

With all the naïveté of a 22-year-old girl, I put on my best dress, hailed a taxi (I did not have a car), and went to my first real interview.

I wasn't really prepared, as I had no idea what kind of job I was applying for. I was told that it would be a great opportunity, especially for a girl. I was interviewed by a man who only asked me a couple of questions. To be honest, I can't even remember what they were, but I do remember that the interview was over quickly, and when I walked out of the office, I had a new job. The pay was a staggering (at the time) $8.64 per hour. I could wear jeans to work, and I would have the opportunity to join the International Brotherhood of Electrical Workers (IBEW). I didn't even know what that was, but he made it sound amazing! Of course, for me to have a permanent position, I had to first make it through a 30-day probationary period, during which I would have on-the-job training. The job was Monday through Friday, 7:30 a.m. to 4 p.m., with weekends off. Hallelujah! No more Saturday working at the restaurant, and I could actually quit my night job at Pizza Hut.

I called my dad and told him that I needed his help buying items for my first real job. He took me shopping where I bought my first pair of steel-toe boots and two pairs of Levi's jeans.

On a Monday morning in April, 1984, I reported to work at the Pennsylvania Electric Company (Penelec) to start my job as the first female groundman in the company's history. I was taken to the dock area, where I was introduced to all the other linemen, shown around the shop, and given a quick lesson on how to determine which crew I would report to each day. My first crew chief was a wonderful man named Bill, and my crewmates were Danny and Eddie. The first few weeks, I felt like I was in heaven. It was fun working outside, and I was learning something new every day. I learned how to drive a stick shift that first week and was also handed my first pair of hooks and a climbing belt. I learned how to drive a truck with a telephone pole attached to a trailer behind me. I was instructed how to back that pole and truck into a field or a narrow alleyway. I learned how to dig a hole, set a pole, climb a pole, work off a set of hooks to frame the pole, hang a cross-arm, hang a transformer, and string lines. Sometimes we did all of that in the middle of the night, whether in rain or snow.

I would learn how to work energized lines, change streetlights, and hang house services. I would be expected to progress through an apprenticeship that would be at least four years long, culminating in the coveted title of Journeyman Lineman. Game on!

I made it through that 30-day probationary period pretty easily, and I was hired on permanently. I was so proud to be the first female to hold this position, and I felt like the sky was the limit. But, like everything in life, surprises abound, and I was in for a few myself. While almost all the men I worked with were easy to get along with and super helpful, I had my share of run-ins with the guys who thought I had no business being a lineman. I had a crew chief who had me hand dig a six-foot hole with a spoon and spade and left me to do it by myself. When he came back to the job site, he told me that I had dug the hole in the wrong spot. I had to fill it back in and start again a foot away. On another occasion, he had me climb up to the top of a pole and wait for instructions then drove away and came back hours later. I was still at the top of the pole, waiting. My thought was, *he is not going to get the better of me* and he didn't.

Every now and then that chief would test me, and each time, I stuck it out. I knew I belonged there, and I knew I could do that job as well as anyone.

Of course, there were many more wonderful experiences than not-so-wonderful ones. I had a crewmate, Phil, who came dressed like me for a Halloween party, complete with Calvin Klein jeans, a wig, and my hard hat. One guy insisted on coloring the tips of his work gloves pink to match my pink nail polish. We got to be so close that one of my mates was almost the *maid of honor* for my wedding!

My crewmates hung dainty curtains in my truck, always remembered my birthday, let me bake them Christmas cookies, and were always teasing me about the fact that my hair barely fit inside my hardhat. I recognized that I was a woman in a man's world, and if some imaginary line was crossed, I had the inner knowing that things were changing for everyone. Some people just needed a little time to adjust, but at the end of the day, I was one of them. We had respect for one another. They taught me well, and I did my job safely and skillfully. I trusted that they would have my back, and I had theirs. It was a very proud day for all of us when I became a Journeyman Lineman—the first ever at Penelec, and I'm pretty sure in the whole state of Pennsylvania.

I was a lineman in Pennsylvania, Southern California, and North Carolina. I have worked snowstorms, tornadoes, earthquakes, and hurricanes. I have climbed hundreds of poles, strung miles and miles of wire, and hot-washed insulators hanging off 350-foot steel towers in the harbor in Long Beach, Ca. I was always the only woman, always respected, and always treated as an equal. My last storm was Hurricane Ivan. I retired from linework at the age of 43.

When we are born, we inhale for the first time, and when we die, we exhale for the last time. I am living my life so the moments between those two miracles—between the breaths—are as amazing as possible.

I realize at this point in my life that my early decisions have shaped the way I live my life. Going to Brazil and learning a new language was instrumental in my being one of the first 30 people hired for a start-up that later became DirecTV Latin America. The skills I learned as a lineman have carried through the years and I am always prepared to pivot. I have great attention to detail, and I usually do the hard thing first. I always have, or find, the necessary tools to do what needs to be done, whether that tool is a hammer or a book. I know I am capable of anything—even when there is no one in my corner—because I have done hard things, and I trust my intuition above anything. I am more than ready for the next chapter.

My advice for the reader: Live your authentic life, take risks, ask questions, choose to see the good in all situations, and be willing to compromise. You are amazing!

## About Vicke

Vicke Marz has been a waitress, the *only* female lineman for three different electric utility companies, in charge of sports and special events programming at DirecTV Latin America, involved in public relations, power grid and substation operations, and tech sales and executive sales with FedEx. She is a passionate traveler on a path of self-discovery that has taken her from the Amazon to the beach, from Pennsylvania to California, and from yoga to plant medicine. While she is still working on what she wants to be when she grows up, she and her husband/adventure partner, Kevin, are the owners and innkeepers at the Victoria Inn Bed and Breakfast, an amazing place in Erie, Pa!

## Connect with Vicke

Facebook: vickemarz

www.victoriainnerie.com

vicke@victoriainnerie.com

# *Stay the Course!*

**Remlee Peck**

"As I change my thoughts, the world around me changes."[11]

Louise L. Hay

You know what? I've realized the major theme for my life should be, *stay the course.* In other words, "Stay strong and carry on no matter what you face. You got this!" Every time I heard those words growing up, I just had to laugh. "Things always work out," my grandmother would tell me. "One way or the other, right?" *Right!* Truth be told, my Gram *was* right! I just didn't believe it then.

Once I turned 60, I became quite philosophical. For some reason, I started remembering more and more things my Gram would say. I don't know how you feel about your grandmother,

---

[11] Hay, Louise L. *Mirror Work: 21 Days to Heal Your Life,* Hay House, Inc. 2016. P. 92

but I always looked up to mine. Actually, I looked down because she was only four-foot, ten inches tall, and I towered a foot over her. Nonetheless, my grandmother was mighty powerful with her words and always gave the best advice.

My Gram was my biggest fan, after my parents of course. She would say things like, "Ha ha, she cried and wagged her wooden leg." and "Oh, for crackin' ice." which I still use to this day. Mind you, some things my grandmother would say didn't make much sense at the time, but they were cute nonetheless and seemed to fit perfectly for the moment. But one thing she said over and over that made sense in my new philosophical way of thinking was "stay the course!" No matter what happened, good or bad, those were her words of advice, "Stay the course, Remlee, just stay strong and carry on. It'll all work out, no matter what."

Doesn't it seem like you can be living your life day after day, putting one foot in front of the other, and then in the next moment, BAM! Something happens and your whole life takes a turn—could be a turn for the worst; a turn for the better; a turn for the unknown; a left turn; a right turn; a U-turn; a complete STOP; or even an entire turn around. Actually, I can say that all these *turns* have played out in my life in one way or another. And I can thank my Gram for the way I handled each one. Let me tell you how it happened for me ...

## A Turn for the Worst

In the summer following my 60th birthday, my best friend in the whole world, my mother, passed away. You talk about *a turn for the worst*. I was devastated and went into quite a sad place for the next few months. Then, one night I had a dream. In that dream, my Gram came to me and said, "Remember what I always told you, sweetheart, just stay the course. Stay strong and carry on!" It was the very next day that I came out of my deep sadness and was able to put a small smile back on my face. I was finally gaining the *Remlee* back that I had buried away in my sadness! Over the next few weeks, I turned my mom's bedroom into my study and gifted her bedroom set to a family friend for her daughter! And you know what? I could hear my grandmother's words in the back of my mind the whole time saying "things will work out, no matter what you face. Stay strong and carry on. Just stay the course, Remlee." And so, I did.

## A Turn for the Better

That Christmas, a guy I had dated in my 30s moved back in town and asked me out! We hit it off once again. I thought maybe this could be *a turn for the better*. And, it was! I got reacquainted with his mom and siblings, and I had a family back in my life. It filled a big part of me that I had been missing since the loss of my mother. And you know what? My Gram's words rang true again, just "stay the course ... everything always works out, no matter what you face." And I was happy it did! My life was back on track.

## A Turn for the Unknown

During this time, I was employed as a school counselor at an elementary center which was about a half-hour drive from my house. It was with much joy that I went about my counseling position and responsibilities every day, and I felt that I was making a difference in the lives of the students. I loved what I did and *thought* I was doing a great job. But one day, I was called into the superintendent's office. I was being questioned over an issue where they felt they were in the right, and I was in the wrong. The meetings that followed over the course of the next few days were quite intense and nerve-racking. I felt like I was on the chopping block, and I was. I had a feeling that it was due to my age and seniority. It took me about 20 minutes after the last meeting ended to decide that I didn't belong there anymore, nor did I want to be employed there any longer. So, the following morning I turned in my letter of retirement, packed up my office that afternoon, and left with a carload of personal possessions that evening. I can't even begin to describe how I felt that night driving home; my life took *a turn for the unknown*. I was numb, but you know what?! Gram's words popped into my head as I pulled into the driveway, "Stay strong and carry on, Remlee, everything will work out, no matter what you face." Even though the journey that night looked like it had no answers, I knew I had done the right thing.

**A Left Turn**

Now, I was left without a job that I truly loved and a path ahead of me that was as clear as mud. Over the next few weeks, I missed seeing the students I loved so much and my teacher friends, and colleagues that I had become so close to all those years. I felt deflated, dejected, and disheartened, not knowing what I was going to do next. But what I missed most was having a purpose in my life. It wasn't in my nature to just sit on the couch and eat bonbons all day and watch the latest soaps, just because I was *retired*. I was a mover and a shaker, but I wasn't moving or shaking anywhere at that point. That is, until a neighbor who lived in the house on my *left*, asked me for a favor. And you know what? Gram's words came true again, "Stay the course, keep strong, and carry on. Everything works out, no matter what you face!" I was grateful I had the drive and determination built in me by now to do just that. And I most definitely did, once again!

**A Right Turn**

The favor my neighbor asked me to do for her that day ended up changing my life. During the afternoon, I was introduced to an amazing group of women entrepreneurs and business owners who were making a difference in their professional and personal lives. I immediately felt at home with them, and it felt *right*. I ended up joining their professional organization and I'm still a member today. Because of that day, I was empowered to open my own life coaching business, Coaching Kids 4 ChangErie, and found the perfect office to rent within two months. And you know what? It felt good that I had stayed the course and didn't give in to just being *retired*. In the back of my mind, I kept hearing my Gram say, "Everything will work out, just stay strong and carry on, Remlee." I was on my way to helping children and their families, just as I had done as a school counselor. I adored being my own boss. It was a feeling of freedom that I hadn't felt in a long time. I loved it!

## A U-Turn

My coaching business was up and running, but I wasn't attracting many client sessions despite my numerous efforts. As it turned out, I decided I needed to make some big adjustments in my coaching journey and execute a quick *U-e* in my way of thinking. What I was doing was just reenacting all those years as a school counselor, consequently not allowing for any new creative energy to flow in with fresh ideas and additional opportunities. So, I began to recreate and reinvent myself, changed the name of my business, and fashioned a whole new perspective on my coaching career. And you know what? It worked! I now call my business Coaching YOU For Change, and I opened the business up to Individuals, adults, and small groups among other things! Once again, Gram came to the rescue with her words of advice and encouragement, "Stay the course, things will work out, no matter what you face!" And it felt good!

## A Complete STOP

Life went along smoothly for the next few years and my coaching business had improved nicely. I continued to date the same guy and I got to travel quite a bit, which was nice. Until one day in June, I fell in my driveway. I fractured my left tibia plateau and for the next three months, my life was spent in a wheelchair. My days at work completely *stopped*. With a lot of support from my guy and my friends, my injury healed well, and I was able to drive four months later. That November, my guy broke up with me. I guess he thought that texting would be a great way to do it. You know what? As devastating as all that was, I managed to stay the course—thanks to my gram—and carried on for another couple of years.

What happened then was quite a shock. It came as that dreaded phone call ... you know the one that wakes you up in the middle of the night with bad news? My precious brother passed away, unexpectedly. It was the night of my birthday. I was devastated. Immediately I thought to myself, *how am I ever going to get through this one, Gram?*

## A Turn-Around

Once again, with the support of my dear family and friends, I was finally able to hear Gram's still small voice in the back of my head saying, "Stay strong and carry on, Remlee, things will work out." And you know what? This one was big, but I managed to *stay the course*. I knew Gram would be proud of me.

What happened over the next six months was amazing! I registered for a semester-long course to become a master gardener, which was always something that my brother and I had wanted to do. My life *turned around*, and I'm happy to report that I am now a master gardener and ready to offer my own herb garden classes. And you know what? I am contemplating what *seeds* to start planting next in my life. You never know what's going to happen when you just *stay the course! Right, Gram? Right, Remlee!*

In the whole of life, here are some things to remember:

- Where you are headed is far more important than what you left behind.
- Keep moving forward and don't look back. There's a reason the rear-view mirror is smaller than the windshield.
- Your past doesn't determine your future, you do!
- It's all about staying positive in your thoughts, words, and actions.
- Do your best to stay strong and carry on no matter what you face.

I owe so much of my adult life to my grandmother's words of advice that got me through each day. Simply put, *stay strong and carry on, no matter what you face.* All you have to do is "Stay the Course!"

I have kept my grandmother's memories alive in these words. Her name was Hannah M. Lee Peck (1891-1979).

## About Remlee

Remlee Peck, MEd, has been an inspiration to individuals of all ages for more than 35 years. She is a personal supporter and advocate for adults, children, families, and small groups in and around Erie, New York, and California. Her experience as a psychiatric social worker, lifelong educator, and school counselor has opened the way for the creation and success of her own business, Coaching You For Change.

Remlee is a life coach who devotes herself to providing support and assistance to people who may be struggling in difficult areas of their lives. She incorporates various mind-body wellness techniques and seeks to provide unique opportunities to keep a positive attitude a constant companion in their lives.

Remlee is also a motivational speaker who offers participants their own Keys for Success. She has led numerous workshops and seminars both locally and internationally on a wide variety of topics.

In addition, Remlee is a volunteer with the Big Brothers/ Big Sisters Program and also with the Highmark Caring Place, A Center for Grieving Children, Adolescents, and their Families. Remlee recently became a master gardener and can be seen volunteering in the school garden program at a nearby elementary school.

**Connect with Remlee**

www.coachingyouforchange.com

https://facebook.com/coachingyouforchange

https://instagram.com/coachingkids4change

coachingyouforchange@gmail.com

# Reinventing Myself – Never Give Up!

## Linda Laird Staszewski

"I can do all things through Christ who strengthens me."[12]

### - Philippians 4:13

As a child, I could often be found hiding behind my mother's skirt. I was pitifully shy. I had one sister, Carol, who was seven years older than me. We loved and supported each other, but we had opposite personalities. She ended up having seven wonderful kids, while we were not blessed with children. Dad was a police officer and Mom a factory sewer of baby clothes. I attended St John Grade School, along with the other neighborhood kids. It was a good childhood. I went to St Benedict Academy, an all-girls high school, as most of my friends were going there. I opted for

---

[12] Phil 4:13 (NKJ)

the business program as opposed to college preparation. I thought I would marry and get a job, which I did, but I never outgrew that craving to learn and grow.

I met my future husband, Tom, when we both worked at a local supermarket: he after school, me after working in an office. I had purchased a new blue stick-shift Camaro convertible using my graduation money as down payment. I strove to pay it off sooner and took a second job. It was there we met, and the attraction was mutual. We dated for five years. Tom graduated from Penn State University. Teaching positions were difficult to find at the time, so he accepted a teaching job in Reading, Pa., which is eight hours away. It was a long year. We married a year later, and I moved to Reading. I was so homesick. I found an office job in a chemical plant nearby, and we lived there two more years before deciding to quit our jobs and move to Pittsburgh, Pa., which was closer to Erie. My dear dad was very ill, and we wanted to be closer to home.

When we moved to Pittsburgh, Tom got a job in administration working at the Community College of Allegheny County (CCAC). I took a job working in the engineering department of a manufacturing company. The department was going through training for a computerized system. I attended classes with the engineers, as I was the one who was responsible for making any necessary changes to the program. The manager asked me to get certified in the program. I kept putting it off, out of fear of not passing the test. When he left for another position, he gave me a frame, in which to put my certificate. I was so moved that he had that kind of belief in me that I took the test and passed it. My confidence grew.

The plant was closing. During that time, it was like going to a funeral every day, awaiting my turn to be let go. It was painful and traumatic for all. The sadness was prevalent, as employees had grown close over the years, and most of us would never see one another again. All lives were in turmoil. One manager friend took it especially hard; he lost his identity along with his confidence. He took another job but found it to be overwhelming, so he quit. Tragically, he ended up committing suicide. We were all in shock.

It was time to move on and get a new job. I landed the job I had wanted for a long time. It was in a beautiful manufacturing facility located on a hill with acreage. The company was German-based and pristine with glazed floors and state-of-the-art equipment. I was hired as a time study technician and was delighted to be employed there. The gist of this position was productivity measurement, workflow, and efficiency. It was an unpopular job, as employees were expected to produce the number of pieces the results of the study proved. It was a boogie-man job and double-so for a woman, especially back then.

I enrolled in the community college, and it took many years of evening classes to attain my associate's degree in industrial engineering production technology. This was a challenge for me, as I was very weak in math. I'd come home from class crying and thinking that I was *slow*. I thought of quitting, but I am persistent and kept on going. It started fitting together, like a puzzle, and I developed the left-hand, logical side of my brain to a degree. This added to my credibility on the job and opened a whole new career for me.

Being a woman in a man's position back then was a true challenge. I was ridiculed and jeered. Whenever I bought a piece of equipment, many stood behind me saying they would not use it and I would be fired. Refusing to be deterred by their comments, I stood stoically, as though I had heard nothing, but my knees were shaking. A few would leave their toolboxes open, allowing nude girly pictures to show. Another chewed tobacco, which was all over his lips. It was rough. I prayed and just kept on going, hiding my emotions.

Then, there was the eight-hour time-study of the assembly of a pump. This is where each and every detailed movement—including parts, tools, and dimensions—everything was written down. It ended up being over eight hours of recording manually! Well, the assembler exaggerated every movement, every process, walking to the warehouse several times, etc. I let him do it and at the end of the day, I showed him the time study sheets, every line filled out, every extraneous movement recorded. I asked what he thought our bosses would say. His friend laughed out loud, saying, "You said she didn't know!" I could have gotten him time off but opted not to. Instead, I cut him a break. I said we would start over tomorrow, with all tools out, all parts there, and no extra trips to the warehouse. He was embarrassed but grateful, as he would have been in a great deal of trouble. The word got out, *she's tough but fair*. No one wants their productivity challenged, and I understood that. I was a threat. I told them if they disagreed with the results of the study, I would redo the study. I never had to. I always endeavored to be fair in everything I did and still do.

After a while, I decided to go back for my bachelor's degree in business management at Carlow University. It would be another five years after that before I returned to earn my master's in professional leadership/organizational development. It was the first time I had ever made the dean's list! Applying myself brought success and increased knowledge. I still look back over the total of nine and a half years of working all day at a grueling job and then going to night school and don't know how I did it. Yes, I do ... God!

Then, I got a promotion to plant engineer, taking on the maintenance of the plant, the HVAC/Heat system, plant layout, working with engineering to build a detoxification room, managing the hazardous waste program, and various projects. I wasn't skilled in mechanics, so I met with the maintenance team telling them just that. We worked together so well as a team: I got the money approved and together with their knowledge, we did it! It was a hard-working group, and I was blessed to work with them.

My right-hand man, Bob, helped me with my credibility. We made renovations to the shop's men's rooms, and in the shop, we added sodium vapor lights to the existing lighting, and numerous ongoing improvements were made. I earned their respect over 17 years.

When I left the company, I felt such ambivalence. We were moving home to care for my beloved mom, as she was top priority. But it was difficult to leave my second family and the friendships created over the years. It was time though.

My beloved dad had passed, and my dear mom was 84 years old, and only mobile with her walker and wheelchair. Being a caregiver was challenging, but it was a labor of love. It was my honor, and I was blessed to be there for her for three precious years, and I am forever grateful for that special time. She passed in our home; I had my hand on her chest telling her it was all right to go to Jesus, and that Dad, and other family were waiting for her. Then, she was gone. I called the family and friends to let them know. It hit me when the ambulance took her away. *Wham!* How I miss her—how I cherish the gifts both parents gave me, in terms of love, strong faith, and belief. Thank you, Jesus, for my family, for the memories, for the love.

I had various jobs in Erie and found one similar to my job in Pittsburgh. I worked there for almost two years and then found myself unemployed.

*Oh no! What am I going to do now?* I was broken, devastated, and depressed. After a successful career as an industrial engineer, I found myself unemployed. Being a positive, onward and-upward thinking person, I searched for another job. I was scared, but after all, I went through evening classes, after working all day, for nine and a half years to attain my master's degree. I had credentials, experience, and references. Surely, I would have no problem. Off I went! Back I came, feeling totally shattered. That's when I realized that companies didn't want me at age 59. I was, in their eyes, close to retirement. I sat and cried, feeling worthless and dejected, aching with the pain, and loss of myself. I prayed to God, as I always do. He smoothed the path before me.

Thank God for my husband of 47 years, the love of my life, my best friend, and my ongoing support system. He calmed me down, reminding me that it would be alright. This took some of the pressure off, and I felt at peace. Financially, I needed to work, and we were used to two paychecks, like most people.

I am resilient. I started over once again at age 66. I reinvented myself, and *this* time, I would do things I had a passion for. This included creativity: arts, crafts, sculpting, jewelry-making, and mentoring others to live their best lives. I wanted to help women escape the stress and relax with other like-minded women, to take time for themselves, and to explore their own creativity. Thus, Escape to Create Workshops was born, offering classes on planning, prioritizing, and achieving goals with vision boards. Also offered were motivational and craft classes, along with private parties for all ages. This concept was very popular and was well-received by attendees. Yet, I had more to give, more lives to touch.

At the age of 67, prayer led me to create DIY Crafts Kit subscriptions, where people could complete an upscale project in the comfort of their own homes. They had access to an online video, too. I dove in! The pandemic left people in need of such projects.

A friend suggested a new idea: I should create gift boxes, which I could personalize, so I did. Queens Comfort Boxes took off immediately. An optional survey on the website allows me to know the recipient's preferences, and I integrate that into her box.

Fast forward to age 71, I read my first anthology book, which is a collection of authors compiled into one book with a specific theme. I'd always toyed with the idea of writing my own book. I started my book, but then life took over, and the project was sidelined.

I enjoyed the idea of short stories of passion, inspiration, and motivation. I wanted in! *Why doesn't anyone start an anthology here?* I thought. The Lord tapped me on the shoulder and said, *why don't YOU?* This spoke to my heart. So, here we are, 20 strong and amazing women, each sharing her story of conquering obstacles, of forging ahead to live her best life, while encouraging and inspiring girls, women, and especially women in their 60s. This is also beneficial to men, who support their wives and daughters.

And *yes*, I still have exciting new ideas and goals planned! It's never too late and you are never too old to become who you want to be. There is so much to do, so little time.

I encourage all to utilize their skills, learn and develop new talents, and explore their creativity. I especially want women over 60 to realize that life begins at 60! You can still attain your dreams and goals. You do not have to retire from life, as this is a time of growth and discovery if you want it. You are *never too old,* and it is *never too late* to reignite your life. Believe in yourself and you will be *unstoppable!*

I am thankful to God, for through Him *all things are possible!* Believe in yourself!

## About Linda

Linda is a retired industrial engineer, vision board guru, multi-business owner, curator, author, creativity coach. She attended evening classes for over nine years to earn her master's degree in professional leadership/organizational development. She is results-oriented and mentors numerous women providing support, direction, and goal setting.

At age 66, she launched Escape to Create Workshops, which includes vision board and craft workshops and motivational webinars

One year later, Linda founded DIY Crafts Kit subscriptions, where customers create upscale do-it-yourself crafts in the comfort of their own homes or in workshops.

She then added Queens Comfort Boxes to her line, which can be personalized via an optional questionnaire. Each gift box is filled with useful and fun items.

At age 70, Linda started a Facebook page to support women over 60, where they can connect with like-minded women, Unwavering Women 60+: "Live Your Best Life!"

She belongs to numerous women's groups, clubs, and organizations where women support and empower one another. She continues to grow, being an advocate of life-long learning. Linda strives to help people of all ages to clarify, plan, set, focus on, and achieve goals.

Linda Laird Staszewski, author and curator of 20 Lives Ignited: 20 Women OVER 60 are Creating their Success on their Own Terms!

**Connect with Linda**

Facebook: Linda Laird Staszewski

strongamazingwomen@gmail.com

www.diycraftskit.org (Queens Comfort Box, *20 Lives Ignited* is on this website)

www.facebook.com/escapetocreateworkshops

20 Lives Ignited

www.facebook.com/20livesignited-lls

www.facebook.com/queenscomfortbox

Unwavering Women 60+: Live Your Best Life: https://www.facebook.com/groups/2872641486340613

# Rising Phoenix

## Women Surviving against the Odds

# *Color Blind*

## Thasia Anne

"Abused women are some of the most perfect women in the world, as they are trying not to be abused again."

- Linda Lyons King, Former Director of SafeNet

In November of 1961, my mother's illness was finally identified. It was the Saturday I turned six.

My mother, Betty Anne, instructed my father, Dick, to have a birthday party for his little girl. I remember it quite clearly. My father invited his buddies over to play poker. One of them brought me a child-size broom and dustpan set. I cleaned up their chip crumbs and brought them beers.

Happy Birthday, Thasia Anne.

When my father learned that my mother would need several months of rehab to live with her new limitations, he left. He drove out of Erie, Pa., with another man's wife and children, and never looked back.

We struggled due to Mother contracting polio, needing rehabilitation, and her husband's departure. We lived in a very Catholic neighborhood, where Mother was the only single woman. We were easily the lowest income family in that area. These events were before the advent of food stamps, healthcare insurance, and other assistance. My mother worked odd jobs, and we found ways to get by.

When I turned ten, my mother met an Andy Taylor-looking guy named Jim. My grandparents had started taking my mother to Civil Defense Commission meetings. Gramma Anne made it clear, "You may have some problems, but there is always someone who has it worse," and encouraged her to take up a volunteer position serving coffee at the Civil Defense meetings.

Jim drank seven cups of coffee in one night just to talk with Mother. Betty Anne didn't quite get his humor early on. She was still reeling from all that had happened to her. Jim kept at it, and eventually, they began dating. They married when I was 14 years old.

\* \* \*

At 15, I met him. He filled my head with platitudes about how wonderful and beautiful I was—that no one else ever understood him. He said that those cautioning me about him were just jealous of our love. I was 15, and he was 22. RED FLAG.

He would say because I was so gorgeous, he could not keep his hands off me. He had to have me. Everything is somehow my fault. RED FLAG. I was in love. I was turned on. I wanted him too and became pregnant at 15. RED FLAG.

My mother was very reluctant but allowed us to marry right after I turned 16. He told them that if they didn't, he would take me to a state where I didn't need their signature. RED FLAG. We got married in a church, in the eyes of God. That's a trap abusers love. RED FLAG.

He started pushing me around and swinging me by my hair. RED FLAG.

It starts very slowly, with lots of love and flowers between flare-ups. What did I know? There were few good times; there were many more bad times. He attempted to take my life.

I kept asking God, *why doesn't he just love me?* I tried to be perfect.

We lived in a very rural area, a common trick of abusers so that victims have no close allies or safety net.

During my stay-at-home-mom phases, he would accuse me of contributing nothing to the household. So, I would get a job, and he would accuse me of cheating on him with anyone. I would quit the job to show him he was the only one. He would start saying I was just lazy and not contributing.

I would get another job. He accused me of having an affair with a delivery man. So, I quit. A short time later, I was fat and lazy again. I weighed around 110 pounds at the time.

**THURSDAY 5:15**

Twenty minutes to four

My make-up was on

Dinner was bubbling on the stove

Wiped my young man's nose

brushed his hair

Changed the baby's pants

Looking at clock

stomach flops 4:04

Kids clean in front of TV

Table is set

Picked up magazines

from living room floor

Panoramic view

everything; tidy and in place

4:30 I had started to finish dinner fixings

Then I stopped

My oldest said "Mom I'm hungry"

I replied, somber, sad

"We have to wait for Dad"

5:05 the baby was crying

I took him to the kitchen

Strapped him in the highchair

My oldest repeated, "Mom I'm hungry"

"I know Honey, here have a bite"

5:15 he tore into the drive

He saw us at the table

"Thanks for waiting Bitch"

20 Lives Ignited

I said in a toneless voice,

"The boys were hungry"

"It was you, ya fat pig

Ya just couldn't wait

Here, eat this ya pig"

My whole pan of stew now spewed across

the cool kitchen tile

He headed to the door, "I'll eat out"

5:17

I weighed myself three times

Scale shows 111 lbs.

Can I be a fat pig at 111lbs?

My brain says no

My heart cries clean up the mess in the kitchen ya pig

* * *

I married him in God's eyes, which meant a lot to me. Therefore, I felt I couldn't just quit. God might be angry with me. After all, it is for better or worse.

I started studying the Bible. I knew if he cheated, I had a biblical way out. I searched and reviewed. I allowed a group to come to my house and study the Bible with my boys and me. I gave one of the ladies riding lessons to explain them being there. However, one of my boys mentioned something innocent that gave away my dastardly plan for my boys to know Jesus. Didn't he marry me in church? But he now refused to allow church ladies in our house to study. So, they parked in my driveway, and we studied in the car. My boys loved Bible time. When he got wind that they were parking in the driveway, he proclaimed that it was his driveway, and they were forbidden to park there. A half a mile away was a game land, my Bible-study partners started parking there, and we walked down once a week for Bible time. I eventually found two passages that set my heart free: "They claim to know God, but by their actions they deny him. They are detestable, disobedient and unfit for doing anything good."[13] (Ti 1:16) and "Fathers, do not provoke your children to anger, but bring them up in the discipline and instruction of the Lord."[14] ( Eph 6:4)

---

[13] Ti 1:16 (NIV)

[14] Eph 6:4 (ESV)

Discovering this allowed me to see the light at the end of the tunnel. We married in the church.

Therefore, he knew God. He was withholding the Lord from our sons just to mess with me. I now had the Lord's armor. He could tell something had changed in me. Of course, he accused me of having someone else. I did, GOD!

Things escalated, and my life was in danger. He held my head underwater in the kitchen sink because dishes were not washed before he arrived home. A week or so later, while driving me to work, he stopped the car, got out, and removed a bayonet knife from his pants. He ran to the back of the car and stabbed both back tires! I hopped out of the car and sprinted toward town. He began to chase me, and I knew I would die.

Instead, I felt almost scooped along and got farther away. I am very short. He is very tall with long legs. When he realized that he couldn't catch me, he stopped, cupped his hands around his mouth and yelled, "Aren't you going to help me change the tires?" The answer was no. I ran on into town. I called the school and told them not to let him pick up our boys, that I was on my way, and there was a family emergency. We bolted the doors and locked the windows. He came after dark and stood staring in the bedroom window all night. The boys were now 15 and eight.

These events were all mid to late 80s, and no genuine care plan existed for abused families. My pay was not enough to pay the bills, but I earned too much for any help. After promising no more drinking and seeking counseling, I let him back in. It only took two weeks to escalate to the point that he was walking around the house with a loaded gun threatening us all in a drunken state.

That night, sitting in the bathtub thinking he would kill me and that the firefighters would find me naked; I felt a nudge from God. I suddenly knew that God did not want me or my children to die for a mistake I made as a fifteen-year-old girl. God saved us that night, and we left for good that morning as soon as the sun came up.

I began documenting my journey through poetry and was guided to take it to the local women's shelter. I fumbled along. At first, I attended group counseling at that shelter, then I ran the group, eventually creating their education department and voluntarily facilitating my program in schools from kindergarten to college. I created a *warning signs* list that I handed out to the kids.

Occasionally I would be out somewhere in a store and a young person would come up and ask, "Are you that woman that came to our school? I gave that list to my sister, and she got away from her bad boyfriend."

I also found that my poetry about that life was making an impact. People were responding.

Without a degree I couldn't get a job helping women, even though I had 17 years of real-life experience. I enrolled in the social work program at Edinboro University of Pennsylvania and received my degree at 60 years old.

For the next five years I worked for a nonprofit that helped single working women with or without children to find safe affordable housing. I began to seek a publisher for my poetry.

Every year in October, which is National Domestic Violence Awareness month, I led walks and read my poetry. One year, my poetry inspired a fellow survivor to write her own story and share it the following year alongside me at the walk. I led awareness events in several communities. Alien Buddha Press published my articles on the topic, and I have two books of poetry on the subject: *Love and Licorice Whips* and *Subtle Shade of Bruise*. You can find most of my books on Amazon under Thasia Anne.

In 2020, I retired and dove head on into my writing. My goal when I escaped, and even now, is to help victims realize that there is life after abuse. You *can* have a great life! Fortunately, I am happily married to a wonderful, sweet man and enjoy life as a writer and encourager.

To date, I have six poetry books, two romance novels, and am featured in ten poetry anthologies.

This is my second invite into a gorgeous and inspiring anthology for women.


**BOLL WEEVIL**, *Subtle Shade of Bruise*, 2019

My soul had been pummeled like a cube steak

Any long gone ego

plucked like a soup chicken

The man I carefully picked

like prime cotton

after weighing all the others

He turned into a boll weevil

feeding on me and my joy

I still look better today

than I did thirty years ago

Where my picture license showed

lifeless eyes

and lackluster hair

He has had five divorces, three long gone live-in's

and is alone today

still wondering why he couldn't find a single good woman

**CLAW CLIMBING,** *Subtle Shade of Bruise,* 2019

I have been climbing

and reaching for answers my whole life

With raw fingers and with dead tired feet, numb

I clawed I scratched

With nothing left to give

I pulled one more time

Heaving breath, eyes closed rest

When I lifted lids and the vision cleared

with senses aware

I realized I am finally here

## About Thasia Anne

Thasia Anne is a social justice advocate, social worker, poet warrior, and great-grandmother of five. She survived domestic violence and has pushed her way to becoming a *thriver*. Thasia leads domestic violence awareness walks, talks, and poetry readings. Her book, *Subtle Shade of Bruise*, allows the reader to experience the totality of domestic violence.

Thasia also produces a cable access television show, *Poetry, Prose, and Personalities* on CAMerie.com, that allows her to bring culture and local creative talent into the homes of those who can't get out.

Thasia Anne facilitates free writing workshops for youth all the way through seniors. In 2021, Thasia Anne was a finalist for Erie County Poet Laureate.

For ten years she produced a live poetry dance production, WOW or Women of Word with a few Man-Made Words. Based on themes ripped from the headlines each year, the poets produced vignettes on subjects such as domestic violence, homelessness, mental health, and many more topics. Dancers interpreted songs in a way that helped the audience empathize with those who struggle.

To date, Thasia Anne has six poetry books, is in ten poetry anthologies, and has two romance novels. This is her second invite into a gorgeous and inspiring anthology for women.

**Connect with Thasia Anne**

www.thasiaanne.com

Facebook: Thasia Anne Lunger; Thasia Anne Poetess/Author Facebook page

Email: tannetaf@gmail.com

# *Behind the Mask*

## Shelley Chicas

"... it's a journey from here to heaven, and it's a good rule of
journeying to travel light."[15]

- M. Scott Peck

There are moments in our lives when an unexpected pivot
happens. We get a phone call, an accident happens, a diagnosis is
given, an act of violence committed; or maybe simply a moment
of truth reveals itself and a catalyst of change is presented. This is
where resilience is found. I found mine when I was held captive
for five hours. But that's not where this story starts and certainly
not where it ends.

---

[15] Peck, M. Scott. The Road Less Traveled and Beyond:
Spiritual Growth in the Age of Anxiety, New York: Touchstone,
1998. p. 87

In 1995, my life felt like a complete facade; one that was beginning to crumble. Here I was getting closer to 40 years old, a mother of four small children—children I had prayed for all my life—and a wife to a deacon at the church where I served as the pre-school supervisor and taught ladies bible class. I was the darling of the elders and was rewarded accordingly with their performance-based acceptance ... until I wasn't.

What they couldn't see then was that I was wearing a mask—one that hid my pain, my shame, and my doubts; one that hid my constant feeling of drowning. I had gotten involved with a man that lived directly across the street from me. My marriage at the time had dried up. All the relationship manuals and self-help books I read, earmarked, and highlighted to no avail, were collecting dust. We were both tired of the strain of trying to balance work, school, church, and children. What started as temporarily sleeping in separate bedrooms while the kids and I had Hepatitis B became our permanent arrangement. But things took a far worse turn than I could have imagined even then.

One night I was leaving the Dollar Movie Theater, my place of solitude. It was the one thing I could afford that provided me some alone time: two hours to enjoy watching a movie, a small Coke, and popcorn that I didn't have to share. With keys in hand headed back to my van, I felt a hand cover my mouth and the strong grip of an arm wrapped around my waist. I could smell cologne and alcohol as I was lifted and carried across the parking lot to my van.

Thrown into the backseat and now able to face the attacker, I realized it was him. (I don't use his name because I do not wish to give him any color or shape in my mind or in my heart. He doesn't get to hurt me anymore). What had started as a flirtation, turned into one of the worst judgment calls I would ever make. It became an obsession for him.

I could see he was wired from cocaine: his eyes were wild, and he was talking feverishly. He was paranoid that if he let me go, I would call the police and he would be sent back to prison. He cried and pleaded with me, hours passing as I was trapped in this deserted parking lot with him.

Finally, he started the car, driving us toward his apartment. I tried to open the sliding side door, determined to jump out of the moving vehicle, only to have him jam the breaks and drag me out of the van where he dug my keys into my neck and dragged me by my legs across the pavement toward his apartment.

Fear gripped me, and I knew if he got me to his place alone that I would not be going home. I was terrified that I would not get back to my children. Fighting exhaustion, I began to scream as though my lungs were on fire, and grab at every shrub that I could anchor myself to, when two men living in the complex could hear our commotion. They quickly jumped over their patio fence to subdue him and tossed me my keys so I could escape. I ran as fast as I could with hands and limbs shaking.

After being held for five hours trying to reason and plead for my release, I headed to the one friend that I knew wouldn't turn me away. I was bathed, bandaged, and covered with a warm blanket to sleep. I just wanted to hide under the blanket and sleep forever, until I had to face the aftermath.

Disruption was an understatement for the hell that was unleashed upon my family and the church. In the aftermath of this brutal attack, my husband was called, and he convinced me to press charges. Sick to my stomach, I found myself in the district attorney's office: a room with posters of the cycles of abuse, taking evidence pictures, turning left, right, and center of my battered body, making sure to get each black and blue mark and the long ugly scratch across my neck made jagged from his key. How did I get here? The fall from grace was a long hard thunk! And to be honest, it wasn't an enormous leap to find myself in such a pit of misery. My early life came packed with plenty of chaos and turbulence. I almost died a couple of times either by my own hand or as a result of unhealthy decisions. To say I've made some poor choices would be an understatement. The consequences I would face now would be costly emotionally, spiritually, and financially. I was damaged goods.

As it would happen, a friend reached out to me about this *program* in Dallas that promised to bring me peace and clarity. It was designed for those who are emotionally stagnant. She was like an Amway salesman in her pitch, but love was her only motive, and I was broken, bereaved, and didn't know how to move forward from the mess my life had become.

She drove me to the hotel, walked me into the lobby, and gave me the slip. I had no clue what to expect. I was motioned to walk down the hall by people I did not know who all were wildly clapping, and it looked like they were clapping for me—and others who looked as duped and dumbfounded as I felt. Upon entering one of the ballrooms, I noticed several adults standing on chairs looking every bit like the Gestapo and two very well-dressed and distinguished-looking men surveying the bewildered in the room like children. I felt very small and very alone. We each took a seat, and I gave sidelong glances wondering what the hell I had gotten into and what

I could possibly have in common with those assembled. There seemed no commonality visible in dress, size, shape, gender, or race. There was one equalizer ... apparently, we were all broken.

There were posters on the wall with slogans like:

- "What I fear ... I create."
- "Fighting old battles ... in new situations."
- "Same action ... Same result."

It was a game-changer. This would be the place where the *mask* was going to be removed and I would go from victim to accountability. I worked harder and dug deeper than I ever had in any counseling situation I was ever in. I unpacked the lifelong baggage that I had brought into every relationship and situation I had been in. I looked at the self-defeating behaviors many of us fall back on to hide our true authentic selves: *not participating, hiding behind judgments, creating a problem, or playing the nice guy.* We played a lot of games reflecting how what we think and feel determines our behavior. Games that revealed how we give out to everyone else before ourselves. We had to agree to not indulge in caffeine, cigarettes, booze, or any drugs as we peeled away at the years and baggage of our lives like onions. We journaled a lot.

My first entry:

Why I named myself damaged goods. Right now, it is because of the way most people are perceiving me as though if you fall from grace, you are eternally damned.

My church family, the school board, certainly my husband, and his superior self-righteousness look at me as though I was damaged and deranged. Damaged because I couldn't handle my loneliness, my isolation, and the facade any longer.

I have been hurt, disappointed, disillusioned, and yes, damaged. Damaged but not beyond repair. Damaged and needing healing. Battle-worn, with battles fought, lost, and won, to identify the character that I have become. I know I have made mistakes, never out of malice or evil intent. There are those who question my integrity as they judge me as morally deficient. "She is beyond help or hope." I must not allow others' perceptions to shape my views. I know with all these dents, flaws, and weaknesses, there is strength and resolve. Strength to start over, faith in God to be able to guide me to a better place, and hope there can be love.

* * *

I graduated from this life-skills course on April 25, 1995. It was the best decision I ever made at the time, and it changed the course of my life, restoring my joy and helping me move forward being my authentic, flawed, and redeemed self. I started by changing my view from what is right and wrong to what *was* working for me and what was not. I was able to identify my problems—and there were many—figure out how I got into situations, and what my choices were as well as the consequences. I had a lot to face and many decisions to make, but I came away with a real sense of grace. I knew God was with me and would bring my children and family out of the darkness. I consequently ended up sending my now ex-husband through the program so we could be on the same page as we led and helped heal our children through a divorce. Forgiveness is a powerful thing. The friend that sheltered me that dark night also followed suit and many of those that went through the program had real breakthroughs and followed dreams they never thought possible. My attacker—after a lengthy and unpleasant legal preceding— was sent back to prison. He served one year.

Many of us are raised by well-meaning but extremely flawed parents who are only mimicking their own flawed parents. Family life is messy, and relationships ride too long on autopilot. I met many people through my training that have been traumatized by abuse, incest, and violence.

Some were just devalued and ignored, not having anyone believe in them. No wonder divorce is prevalent, drug abuse rampant, and society so seemingly apathetic. We see how hurt people end up hurting people. Real change can happen when we carefully evaluate what works, what serves us, and brings us closer to our goals. It takes a lot of work to break old patterns of behavior. Having true relationships and community happens only when we're willing to be vulnerable and transparent.

The incident in this chapter is only a sliver of my life, having experienced highs and lows prior to and since then. But at this age, this wonderful vantage point that years bring, I am confident in the woman I have become and make self-care a priority. It is better to give out of a full cistern. I have forgiven myself for my inadequacies, never wasting energy on regrets of *if only*. I don't hold back expressing love or encouragement and think twice before I use criticism.

I live gratefully. I am having the time of my life being married for 25 years now to a man who is extraordinary in that he lives *on* purpose and *with* purpose. We have fun. My children are my biggest blessing. I love, like, and deeply respect each one of them.

My grandchildren teach me to live now. My friendships bring me joy, companionship, and color my world. I left the mask-wearing days behind and enjoy the sunshine on my face now.

## About Shelley

Photo by Megan Lyn Photography

Shelley Chicas is an expert in early childhood development and education, with a career that spans over 30 years teaching and promoting literacy in Houston, Texas. She has taught language arts, mathematics, music and movement, and art, and has developed new programs and courses for schools throughout her tenure.

Her passion for children's literacy has taken her to countries across the globe such as India, Honduras, and Mexico engaging in her fierce dedication to volunteer work. She has visited countless orphanages, where she has taught literacy programs and helped build school facilities.

She has also had the pleasure of traveling with medical teams such as Smile Train, World Mission, and House of Charity. These missions aided children with cleft palates and burn injuries, as well as volunteering with W.I.N.G.S. India Foundation, where she has visited with lepers.

Shelley is a proud mother of four, grandmother of five, and a friend to all. She lives in Los Angeles, CA, with her husband.

**Connect with Shelley**

shelleychicas@yahoo.com

https://www.facebook.com/schicas1

https://www.instagram.com/shelleychicas/

# The Warrior Within

## Bonnie Conley

"There is an appointed time for everything. And there is a time for every event under heaven."[16]

- Ecclesiastes 3:1

It all started with a dream.

My parents divorced when I was about six years old. When I was 12 years old, my mother moved to California. In the summer, before my sophomore year of high school, I went to live with my father and stepmom in Pennsylvania. After a little while, I made some friends in the neighborhood. One day, while at my friend's house, her brother had his friend over who just happened to live two houses down from my dad's house. He was the boy next door, literally. When I was about 16 years old, I had a dream

---

[16] Eccles 3:1 (NASV)

about this man whom I had met the previous summer. Little did I know he would become my future husband.

Through a series of events, and a few years later, we both ended up in California. We started dating in the spring of my senior year of high school and got married in the fall of that year. A few years later, we started a family, and my daughter was born in 1981. By 1988, we had four children: one girl and three boys. My husband was now in a partnership with his own business. It wasn't until my youngest one was in middle school, that I decided I wanted to go back into the workforce.

Timing is everything.

I tried different jobs over the years, but they weren't satisfying. Eventually, I joined a local contractor working as a painter but was limited in my creativity due to a lack of services offered. About a year later, I went to work for someone different and had more opportunities to be creative, expand, and learn. I saw a real need for a woman-owned company in this field. So, after a couple of years of working for other contractors, an opportunity arose where I could become self-employed and still collect unemployment. Now was the perfect time to start my painting and handy ma'am business, and in 2004, Bonnie's Finishing Touches was born.

During that same time, the stock market wasn't doing well, so we decided to invest in some rental properties. I figured I could work on them during the winter when business was slow. I was just starting, trying to get my name out there, little did I know both businesses would become full-time jobs.

It was tough going at first. It was a challenge, but I was determined. My husband was self-employed and able to help and encourage me through it. I joined a referral network, and a friend designed a website for me. Within a few years, things were picking up and my business was growing. Life was good. God was good.

I was the first woman-owned painting and handyman business in the area at that time; and in 1999, when I got my motorcycle license, there weren't many women driving motorcycles. I was a trailblazer for sure! I was finally doing things I loved. Seeing the smiles on my customers' faces and a job well done gave me great satisfaction. Things were going well.

It was an early morning in April 2008, and at first, I wasn't sure. Am I dreaming? But there it was again. I was sure I heard something. It sounded like a knock. I finally rolled out of bed and went to explore. There was a knock at the front door. When I opened it, there stood a state trooper. *Oh no, was our son in trouble again? What did he do this time?* But it was far worse than we could have possibly imagined.

Just a few days earlier, we celebrated my birthday with all four of my kids.

Shawn was our oldest son and was diagnosed with attention deficit hyperactivity disorder (ADHD) at a very young age. He seemed to always be getting in trouble and picking on his siblings. As he grew older, he learned to deal with it, but he was easily distracted, to say the least. He had gone out earlier that evening with his girlfriend, and Jack and I had gone to bed. The state trooper proceeded to tell us that Shawn died in a car accident. It was still early in the morning, and we weren't even aware that he wasn't home. It was so surreal, *Oh Lord no, no, no this can't be!* We were devastated, to say the least.

I would have despaired had I not believed "... that I would see the goodness of the Lord in the land of the living."[17] (Ps 27:13) If it wasn't for our faith, I don't know how we would have made it through. But God reminded me of his promises, "'For I know the plans I have for you,' declares the Lord, 'plans to prosper you and not to harm you, plans to give you hope and a future.'"[18] (Jer 29:11)

A few years passed, and we were trying to cope with the loss of our son. Meanwhile, my other son, who was only 15 months younger than his older brother, began showing signs of depression. We really didn't know what was going on at the time.

---

[17] Ps 27:13 (NASB)

[18] Jer 29:11 (NIV)

We later realized it was post-traumatic stress disorder (PTSD) because his brother's death was so devastating to him. A couple of years later, he ended up getting in a motorcycle accident, and fortunately survived, but suffered some mental and physical damage.

Even in the midst of these trials, my husband and I tried to find hope and joy. We were empty nesters and wanted to enjoy the life we had, especially because of what had happened. There are no guaranteed tomorrows. Life became more precious, and we wanted to enjoy the moments we had together. As the years went by, we began to experience joy once more and no longer felt under the weight of grief. Life was coming back into our spirits and hearts. But then ...

Our oldest, our daughter, graduated from nursing school in the spring of 2012, and we were so proud of her. As a single mom, she had worked hard to achieve her goal and raise two kids. Shortly after graduation, she got a job at a nursing facility. She loved the people and they loved her. The following year, she was finally able to get the job she wanted full-time with benefits and was so happy and excited.

Due to an early snowstorm that year, my daughter's car was in an accident. While she was between vehicles, her fiancé's mom would give her a ride to work, and her father would pick her up. Little did my husband know, one night when he dropped our daughter off at home, it would be the last time he would see her.

It was about a week before Thanksgiving, and we were busy making plans for the holiday. We were looking forward to getting together with our children and grandchildren. As my husband and I were getting ready for the day, my son called to tell us his sister died of a drug overdose. It was fentanyl. He had picked up the two kids earlier because they couldn't get a hold of us. So, in November of 2013, the day before Thanksgiving, we were having a funeral service, once again, for one of our children. *Not again Lord, how could this be? Don't they say lightning never strikes the same place twice?*

Our daughter had two children that were ten and 11 years old at the time, and their father was in jail. We were enjoying our years after raising our four children, but what were we to do? Put them in foster care, hoping the system keeps them together? After much thought and prayer, we decided to raise our two grandchildren. This was no easy task and was a really hard adjustment for us. I was self-employed and my husband was working second shift. All of the responsibilities of caring for the grandchildren fell on me. We kept them in their current school for the rest of that school year. It was challenging for me to do my job *and* worry about taking and picking up kids from school. Fortunately, my son lived in town and could pick them up, give them something to eat, and keep them at his place till I could pick them up after work. That was a huge help. It's been a little over nine years since that tragedy, and a lot has happened, both good and bad.

I had to learn to be brave, to move forward one step at a time, even when I didn't feel like it nor wanted to. I had to learn to get back up and fight when I fell down, or when life knocked me down. It's ok to fall. Life has its ups and downs, but when we get knocked down, the trick is not to linger there. Rest for a while, yes, but don't stay too long. Fight to get back up even if it's just one step at a time. Be courageous, be a warrior.

Life is a journey, and we never know where it will take us. With all that has happened to me, I have learned that we must redeem the time God gives us. We are not promised tomorrow. People, be wise today because you don't know how much time you have. My son was only 23 years old when he passed away and had a whole life ahead of him. He never expected this. We always think it won't happen to us, but we are not guaranteed tomorrow. Life is short and precious.

"Be very careful, then, how you live—not as unwise but as wise, making the most of every opportunity, because the days are evil."[19] (Eph 5:15-16)

Now and again, we are bound to experience feelings of fear, failure, or depression, but God doesn't want us to be trapped by the hurts we have suffered. He wants us to be brave, to move on,

---

[19] Eph 5:15-16 (NIV)

and to have hope, "... suffering produces perseverance; perseverance, character; and character, hope."[20] (Rom 5:3-4)

Joy is a choice; we *can* choose it. We attract what we think and surround ourselves with, whether that is peace or anxiety. We determine the atmosphere by what we carry in our spirit. That is why how we think and express our feelings is so important. What are you attracting to yourself?

Be a warrior. Be fearless. Be brave. Courage is not the absence of fear but doing it in spite of the fear. Keep going, don't give up. The answer to your troubles could be right around the corner. After all, the goal isn't to relive the past, your goal is to go forward, toward something altogether new and lovely. "Behold, I am doing a new thing ..."[21] (Isa 43:19)

God blesses us to bless others and comforts us to comfort others, "... who comforts us in all our troubles, so that we can comfort those in any trouble with the comfort we ourselves receive from God."[22] (2 Cor 1:4)

---

[20] Rom 5:3-4 (NIV)

[21] Isa 43:19 (ESV)

[22] 2 Cor 1:4 (NIV)

## About Bonnie

A true pioneer.

After working several years for other contractors, Bonnie saw a real need for a women-owned painting and handyman business. So, in 2004, Bonnie's Finishing Touches was created, and it was the first woman-owned painting and handyma'am business in the area. Their motto is "We create beauty. One home at a time."

Bonnie found her niche and enjoys seeing smiles on her customers' faces. She also started buying and managing rental properties at the same time.

In 1999, Bonnie got her motorcycle license. She was a real trailblazer! As such, she also became a certified scuba diver, a published author in the international library of poetry, and was a background actor, with her granddaughter, in the movie *Shooting Heroin*. Bonnie was the coordinator of the Mothers of Preschoolers (MOPS) children's program in her area for several years.

Bonnie also enjoys gardening and being outdoors. She loves training and competing with her two dogs Bailey and Casey and has been married for 42 years to her best friend, and partner in crime, Jack.

**Connect with Bonnie**

https://www.bonniesfinishingtouches.com

www.facebook.com/bonniesfinishingtouches/

bonniesfinishingtouches@gmail.com

# *Finding Me*

## A Story of Denial and Survival

## Susan Nyberg Dunton

"We must be willing to get rid of the life we've planned, so as to have the life that is waiting for us."

- Joseph Campbell

"What's the difference?" I asked, "Getting the results in my kitchen or in your office?" The audacity, asking me to wait another week to schedule an office visit after already waiting a week since the biopsy. It was a nightmare: lying face down— without the comfortable headrest you'd see on a massage table— my neck was wrenched, and my breasts hung through the cutouts. The nurses tried numerous times to coordinate the screen image with my breast, desperately trying to find the marker. After more than an hour, I raised myself off the table and was helped to a chair. As if I was starring in a cheap horror film, directly in front of me I saw my blood dripping from the table I'd just vacated.

Little did I know that biopsy was just the beginning of a cascade of unexpected life events for me. I started to take a good hard look at my life. I married my high school sweetheart, had three beautiful children, and shared ownership of a successful printing and mailing business with my husband for over 28 years. We were two lonely teenagers who accidentally found each other. I was an insecure codependent, and he was an insecure introvert. It was a storybook romance they said would never last, but we were determined to be together and married at age twenty-one. We were happy and life was good for many years, but the marriage was not set on a firm foundation and, eventually, cracks began to form.

When I was younger, I was a well-behaved girl who always smiled and got good grades, but I was quiet and afraid of being alone. For as long as I can remember, I was always put together and appeared to be happy. I was a perfectionist who couldn't relax and always had a list or ten to accomplish. I was that mom who did it all, so much so that my daughter's friends called me Martha, referring to Martha Stewart. I hosted every holiday and family event, created everything from pillows to costumes, and planned elaborate birthday parties. I was proud to be the local *Martha*. If anything or anyone was broken, I could fix it or them. I planned to be the perfect wife and mother with the perfect house and the perfect life.

My closest friends were not looking through the same rose-colored glasses I was and referred to my life as *Susie Land*. I loved living in *Susie Land*. Even when things were far from perfect, I was hell-bent to fix them and remain in the comfort of *Susie Land*. A lot of it was good, but a lot was not. Nobody knew that I drove to work in tears most days. Nobody knew my husband was verbally abusive. Coincidentally, my dad and my husband's dad were both verbally abusive alcoholics which might explain my husband's behavior and my co-dependency.

Who in their right mind would give up on a 40-year relationship? Not me. My husband became increasingly angry, his drinking escalated, and he distanced himself from me more and more. I convinced myself it was just another rough patch. With the marriage circling the drain, the best outcome for our shared business was to sell it. Everything needed fixed: the husband, the marriage, and the business. It never occurred to me that Susan might need to be fixed. Absolutely not. I just needed to make new plans. If, and when, the marriage and business both ended, I would be OK. As soon as I finished another spectacular Christmas, I'd be free to start my new life. Then, out of nowhere, *bam!* I was diagnosed with invasive ductal carcinoma. That really didn't fit into my plans.

Decisions had to be made. First, I knew I couldn't go through divorce and cancer simultaneously, so I told myself it was God's plan to mend our marriage. Secondly, I had to choose my course of treatment. I decided to have a bilateral mastectomy. A lumpectomy meant radiation and after watching what that did to both of my parents, I was more terrified of that than surgery. I also chose reconstruction because I couldn't fathom having no breasts. Surgery was a disaster. I was allergic to the morphine and had to have an emergency second surgery for a hematoma. I was in more pain than I could have imagined. When I came home from the hospital, I was genuinely surprised that I was unable to take care of myself. As I sat nearly naked in my bathroom with my sister and daughter scrambling to help, I remember looking in the mirror and feeling it was surreal. I spread my arms to provide access to the drains my sister was attending and was horrified at my bruised body. It literally looked as if someone had beaten me with a ball bat.

Weeks passed but the pain did not. It was six long months waiting for the expanders to be removed and the implants inserted. I found out too late that more innovative doctors didn't double their billing with expanders. The high risk for pain was never disclosed to me, and the level of discomfort was extreme. I was left with no choice but to sit and think. If I'd not been forced to slow down and spend time on the porch looking at the birds and trees and myself, I wonder how many more years I would have lived in denial.

As if the physical pain wasn't enough, my idea that the cancer would somehow mend our marriage was far from reality. It didn't take long to see that I was alone, and I wasn't sure which was worse, the physical pain or the emotional pain. Either way, it hurt.

Life had thrown just about everything at me, and so much of what I'd known was gone. With the business sold, my breasts removed, my marriage disintegrating, and my home transformed into a battlefield, I didn't know who I was. My feminine, professional, and personal identities were all in peril. On top of all that, I was grieving the death of my favorite dog who died three days before the surgery. In a matter of months my life was turned upside down. I was lost, and I felt like a failure. *Susie Land* was unraveling.

I fell into a deep depression which the doctor said was due to the trauma of the surgery. I think it might have been the reality I'd avoided for so long. I entered counseling for several years. I started peeling back all the layers of my life, and more importantly, started learning to take care of myself. For someone like me, a caregiver and an excellent co-dependent surviving only to please everyone else, it was a monumental task. I only knew how to be someone's wife or mother.

The implants were not what I expected. I thought they would be attractive and symmetrical. They were rippled, asymmetrical, and hideous. After all that planning, all that pain, and over a year of recovery, I needed to find a new doctor to try to make them right. When I did, he said they were the worst he'd ever seen. I couldn't wrap my head around more surgery, and my husband and I were too busy finding new homes so we could start living solo lives. So, follow-up surgery had to be put off for a while.

Bankrupt emotionally and concerned for my financial security, I started to search for a new job and a new identity. I had a killer resume and all the confidence to go with it. I'd been a small business owner and held numerous nonprofit positions. There was never any doubt I would land a great managerial position. Surprise! Nobody wanted to hire the 58-year-old woman when there were much younger applicants.

Without permanent employment, I figured it was a good time for the follow-up surgery to correct the botch job on my chest. What was supposed to be one surgery turned into four. Not in my wildest dreams did I ever expect that. I often wished I'd never chosen the initial surgery, but maybe that's why I lived when so many of my friends did not.

After being separated for three years and desperate to move on, I finally filed for divorce. The counselor warned me it would take years to get over my long relationship, but I didn't believe her. Turns out, she was right. Divorce didn't mean I could turn off those feelings like one turns off water.

Physically healed, but spiritually and emotionally a work in progress, I was determined to reinvent myself and become a necessary and valuable human being. My life and future were uncertain, but I held my head high and reminded myself daily I was lucky to be alive and grateful for my possibilities, my children, and my experiences. I decided I needed a geographical change. So, I planned to sell my condo and move to Florida where my sister lived. After I put everything in storage and moved out, the deal on the condo didn't close, so there was no payout. I moved anyway because I was sure it would eventually sell.

After six months, I knew Florida was not for me. It was difficult staying positive when nothing seemed to go as I'd hoped. But then, one evening I finally started to rely on faith instead of plans. I remember lying on the guest bed, looking up at the ceiling, and saying out loud, "Now what the hell are you going to do Susan? Gee, do you think maybe you should be a realtor?" It was something I'd always wanted to try. And why had I never done it? I had so little confidence in myself that I'd listened to other people's opinions letting them decide my destiny.

I had two things going for me, perseverance, and hope. The condo never sold. So, I came home, pulled everything from storage, and moved back into my condo. I quickly got my real estate license and achieved a million dollars in sales my first full year. I was hungry to succeed and was up to two million dollars in sales before long. There were plenty of unforeseen obstacles in my path, but I made the journey and found myself and my voice. I was no longer that scared little girl, and I was not a failure.

Years later, I couldn't shake the feeling that I needed to get rid of the implants. After all the surgeries, I asked myself over and over why I wanted them out. It was as if God patted my shoulder to reassure me that I was ready. I was done living with indecision and listening to other people. I was unwavering. I scheduled the surgery and felt totally comfortable with my decision. My son accompanied me to the procedure. When it was over, he entered the recovery room and told me that my surgeon had shared some shocking news. One of the implants had ruptured and was green and toxic. The doctor went on to say that he had been perplexed by my decision to remove the implants I'd worked so hard to perfect. But, when he realized the damage during surgery, and the dire consequences, he was relieved I'd made that decision.

It took a lifetime to have the confidence to listen to myself, but I finally did. And my story hasn't ended. That's the thing about stories, they don't end. The journey continues to evolve. We all have a story, but what sets us apart is how we choose to write the final chapters. I learned to appreciate where I'd been and trusted myself to get where I needed to be. It's not *Susie Land*, and I'm far from perfect, but I am blessed and living as a proud survivor.

## About Susan

Susan Nyberg Dunton is the mother of three adult children and Nana to her granddaughter, Blake. She is a realtor and author of her first children's book, *Can I See My House?* and lives in Erie, Pa. With her bachelor's degree in business education, she taught briefly before owning and operating a small printing and mailing business for 28 years. Susan was also an advocate for anti-bullying for over ten years as secretary, vice president, and president of the nonprofit, The Ophelia Project. She has been a long-time member of the Coffee Club Divas, a women's empowerment group. Creative gifting and gift wrapping brings her joy, as well as decorating and crafting. She also loves cooking, baking, and traveling. Ultimately, her favorite time is spent with family.

## Connect with Susan

skdunton@gmail.com

www.susanduntonbooks.com

# Rise Above and Smile

## Tharifa Wenrich

"The survival of the fittest is the ageless law of nature, but the
fittest are rarely the strong. The fittest are those endowed with the
qualifications for adaptation, the ability to accept the inevitable
and conform to the unavoidable, to harmonize with existing
or changing conditions."

- Dave Smalley

The thoughts raced around my head through the shock of the
impact, *why was this happening to me? I am a good person.* I ran to
the bathroom and looked at myself in the mirror. My whole face
was swollen. My jaw was obviously broken, severely shifted to
one side of my head. I said to myself, *my life is over. I will never be
the same.* I knew I did not deserve what was happening to me. So
why was I allowing it to happen? I rationalized it. He and I had
great moments together. We traveled and things were wonderful
in the beginning. "It only happens when he drinks, that is when
the mental and physical abuse happens." The jealousy, rage, and

controlling behavior are fueled by alcohol. I rationalized it, even protected him by giving a false story to the doctors about my injuries. I was in the hospital for a week and my jaw was wired shut for the following three months. I made excuses for another year before I decided enough was enough. During this time, through all this trauma, I had a great job and loved what I did for a living. I was a personal stylist for celebrities and an entrepreneur in Vancouver, Canada. Most would say I was a successful person.

I did not know then what I know now. Connecting the dots backward, I was living a life of cyclical behavior that stemmed from my childhood. I did not feel worthy, and I settled for less than what I deserved. This pattern was very familiar to me, although at the time I didn't see the connection.

Growing up in Singapore, I was the youngest of seven children. Our parents often fought. Their marriage was always rocky, and the environment was unhealthy. My father was a controlling womanizer who had several extramarital affairs. My mother, on the other hand, always wanted to help others. She had an entrepreneurial spirit and made her own natural medicines for the sick. She always encouraged us to eat healthy and use natural medicines.

At school, I was teased for my skin color and called names. I felt ugly, insecure, and I did not believe in myself. My father encouraged me to play sports, and it turned out to be a great outlet for me. I took solace in participating in sports. I played softball, field hockey, and ran track and field. With my focus on the activities instead of my home life, I excelled and received many medals and recognitions for my achievements.

My passion for fitness and health continued into my 20s. I was doing fitness group demonstrations and promoting healthy living at hotels and community centers to encourage folks to exercise regularly. I gained confidence, and my discipline was noticed by the gym manager. He wanted to train me to compete in the national bodybuilding competition. After six months of training, I won the title of National Champion and got to compete in the World Women Amateur Body Building Federation as part of the International Federation of Body Builders (IFBB) competing against 39 other countries! At the time, I was dating my first husband and he gave me the love I was seeking. He was ten years older than me and a very successful businessman. I think I was seeking a father figure and he fit the bill. He ultimately betrayed me, having multiple affairs during our short marriage.

I began to experience crippling anxiety soon after, causing me to be hospitalized. I also found out I was pregnant and gave birth to a beautiful baby boy, Kyle. I eventually began a new relationship and had a 15-year-long marriage with a man who adopted my son. Over time, it was apparent that my second husband was not happy with himself or his career. He began a cycle of drinking, investing and losing money, and was diagnosed bipolar. My husband betrayed my trust, just in a different way than in the previous relationship.

Kyle was 16 years old after the second divorce and he said something to me that lit me up in the best of ways. He said, "Mom, I just want to tell you how great you are. No matter how far you fall, you always rise above and smile." This was a monumental moment for me. I always felt I was a failure at life, even though I got stronger with every challenge. I always figured things out on my own as a single mom. From that moment on, I made the decision to be the best version of myself and continue to make my son proud. I wanted to break the cycle.

After some time, I realized that I needed to focus on me. I was turning 50 years old and planning a trip with my sisters to celebrate my birthday. On the one hand, I was very excited to get away, but on the other hand, I had a terrifying feeling about turning 50. My emotions were like the ocean in motion. I was calm, then suddenly, a tidal wave hit me. After two failed marriages and one extremely toxic relationship, I asked myself, *now what?* I meditated often, thinking of what I wanted my life to be. Am I going to be alone for the rest of my years? Where will I retire? Who will be my circle of friends? Would I still live in Canada with the cold winter weather every year? Would I still be healthy?

At the time I was comfortable; I loved my job as a stylist but felt something was missing. I decided that I wanted to live on a tropical island, meet a man whom I could laugh with, and one that shows respect. This was my vision and my dream. I decided to go to Hawaii for my birthday trip. It was there that I met my husband. I felt drawn to him in a way I couldn't explain. I thought *I have prayed for this. Could this be it? He has great manners, and we have fun together. Did I manifest a life partner?* Turns out, I did! We dated long-distance for a year, then got engaged. After 30 years in Canada, I made the move to Hawaii, where I still live now in a happy and healthy marriage.

My goal to become a lifestyle coach emerged from my own life experiences, good and bad. I have invested in myself, and personal development freed me from being a mental slave.

These experiences were not mistakes, they were lessons learned and were the fuel I needed to break the cycle. The cycle of believing in and buying into conditions and beliefs that weren't serving me. I realized I was attracting these circumstances, without even knowing it. I can speak about it now with confidence and conviction because I have done a lot of inner work with mindset training. Thinking back on my life, there are several moments that triggered my body to experience anxiety: starting a new job, starting a new relationship, getting on a plane, unkind people, and when I did not produce the results that were *expected* of me. I was very determined to control these feelings. I used deep breathing exercises, meditated, and watched comedies to distract myself. I tried everything!

I found a breakthrough for treating anxiety. I tried CBD because it was natural and did not have the side effects of pharmaceutical drugs. I always had a passion for natural healing instilled in me by my mother. I researched and read testimonials about how the products helped those suffering with anxiety like I did. I started to notice that I felt better, slept better, and I just felt different in so many ways. Within a month and a half, I noticed my feeling of panic was decreasing. This was a defining moment in my life. I ultimately decided that this was my life mission, to dedicate myself to helping others control their anxiety and not let anxiety control them. For the past three and a half years, I have helped thousands of people begin to heal their anxiety and have a better quality of life. Inner work, mindset, and CBD helped me find the balance between mind, body, and soul.

I have a mission to guide those like me, living in fear and with anxiety, in unhealthy environments. My message is that there is hope and a solution. It doesn't matter your age. You can have the best life imaginable. You can live a healthy lifestyle, pain-free. You can travel the world. You can dress the way you want and not worry about what others say about you. You can speak your mind if you have an idea. You can live anywhere in the world you desire. You can be adventurous. You can fail at something, and it'll be ok. You can be a good wife, good mother, good daughter, and good friend. You can start your own business without any degrees. You can find the soulmate that you dream about. You can be confident, take chances, be pain-free, and not be controlled by the programs that were instilled in you. If you ever doubt these things, think about my story. I am living proof. If I can do it, you can too!

## About Tharifa

Tharifa Wenrich is a mother, wife, and grandmother who currently lives in Hawaii. She began her career as a flight attendant, traveling the world. Tharifa's career expanded to fashion stylist for celebrities and entrepreneurs in Canada. She also worked in a modeling agency, helping women in grooming and personal deportment.

Tharifa has always had a passion for health and fitness. Her fitness goals have followed her into her 50s, as she was a fitness competitor in the 2017 Hawaii National Physical Competition. She also participated in the Ms. Health and Fitness Competition and raised $15,000 for Wounded Warriors.

Tharifa has experienced crippling anxiety throughout her life. Being a lifelong health and wellness advocate, she decided to address her health struggles by utilizing holistic medicine. She has studied chi nei tsang and an ayurvedic lifestyle which helps bring people's minds, bodies, and spirits to balance.

Tharifa studied the Thinking Into Results (TIR) Program with the Proctor Gallagher Institute. This program teaches about mindset and how it affects wellbeing. She practices and applies the skills she has studied while actively participating in a weekly TIR mastermind meeting with other entrepreneurs.

Having gained an enormous amount of skill and experience during her personal transformation, she is able to help many of her clients reclaim their goals with regard to health, wellness, fitness, relationships, and career paths, becoming a better version of themselves. Tharifa now helps others transform in their personal journeys.

Tharifa also has a shopping network business where she guides her clients in the use of natural products in their daily life.

**Connect with Tharifa**

https://mydailychoice.com/healingelement

http://www.babetteryou.com

https://www.facebook.com/tharifa

https://www.facebook.com/hempworxoahu

# Setting the World on Fire

## Women Impacting Globally

# *Thriving Beyond Anxiety*

## Tarnie F. Israelsson

"We can never obtain peace in the outer world until we make peace with ourselves."[23]

- Dalai Lama

Safety was not a feeling I knew—not in my childhood, nor for many years after. I lurched myself from one anxious moment to the next, stuffing down my fear to try to show up for my life. Underlying my constant anxiety was a feeling of not being good enough. It was not until I was in my 30s that I knew this was the core belief underpinning my life. I didn't know that I longed to feel safe, to feel supported, to be seen, and be loved.

Today, I realize my anxiety kept me from enjoying many things in my life. Paradoxically, it also helped me achieve what I am doing today. I have come to view this aspect of myself as a gift.

---

[23] https://thedailymind.com/the-dalai-lama-what-can-he-show-you-about-peace-at-work/

Let me explain.

From the age of 14, I decided I wanted to be a sports medicine physiotherapist (aka, physical therapist). I thrived on working with the athletic population who were committed to their own healing. By the age of 28, I had my own practice in Sydney, Australia, Mosman Physiotherapy and Sports Injury.

Working with the physical body, I increasingly noticed that clients would bring up emotional issues which were seemingly connected to whatever body issue we were treating. While I was treating their lower back, or neck, or knee, they would share their relationship issues, how depressed they felt, and tell me about their fears. By my early 30s, I was drawn to study psychological practices to support the healing my clients sought. My exploration eventually brought me to Los Angeles to study psychology.

Not surprisingly, my journey to learn how to heal others opened the door to my own healing.

During the first half of my life, I rarely felt safe. My underlying anxiety was debilitating at times. In the first few months of starting my master's degree in psychology, a friend and fellow student turned to me as we were hiking in the Santa Monica mountains and said, "I think you are suffering from anxiety." She had similar issues and had been diagnosed, but I had not. I didn't know what it was.

Tarnie F. Israelsson

My anxiety showed up in many different ways: I was afraid of driving, riding in elevators, or going to new places. I didn't want to be alone or be on my own, and I was always looking to someone else for validation. I often felt intimidated and hated being noticed yet longed to be seen. I was constantly worried about being criticized or judged, to the point I was getting stomach aches.

I lived in fear that I was getting it all wrong—everything. I often felt I was not taken seriously and that nobody listened to me. I berated myself for not being important enough, good enough, intelligent enough, worldly enough, pretty enough, articulate enough, and the list goes on. This and more kept me disconnected from my body because deep down I held a belief that I didn't belong, anywhere and everyone was better than me.

These anxious thoughts were not only affecting me mentally, but they were also encroaching on my physical health. In my late 20s, I was slightly overweight and had severe stomach aches. As a ten-year-old, my appendix was removed to *fix* this, but nothing changed. I also suffered from sinus allergies, sluggishness, brain fog, fatigue, and a recurring neck and arm tingling pain that stopped me from playing competitive tennis, which had been a significant part of my life. I could feel I *wasn't right*. I attributed my symptoms to long hours of physical work.

Incredibly, at the same time, I was treating a middle-aged tennis player for a hamstring injury. As she described her

169

symptoms, my first thought was, *they are mine too!* After consulting with an osteopathic doctor, I began addressing my physical issues, including radically changing my diet. Gradually, I began to feel healthier, more alive, vibrant, and full of energy, which thrust me into the exploration of healing modalities that included somatic healing practices.

Within months of completing my MA in Applied Psychology, I attended a somatic-based movement class. After ten minutes of moving, I had a profound experience of *I am home* as tears ran down my face. The joy of feeling present in my body was exquisite and a totally new experience for me. It had taken me six months of knowing about the class before I was ready to attend, because I was so afraid to go.

Building on the foundation from my university training and working with other mentors, the somatic movement certification was life changing. This training gave me the gift of birthing my own somatic-based healing practice: Body Centered Method™.

My childhood experiences of living with a violently eruptive alcoholic father and a fearful and critical mother, created a deep internal terror which left my nervous system on high alert. I never knew what I would get at any moment—a nasty criticism, a scream, a threat of being hit, and at times, I feared I might die.

While there were wonderful times growing up on a sheep property in the mountains of New England in New South Wales,

Australia, there were many times I felt myself pushed into the wall (metaphorically), disappearing to get away from the terror and violence in the living room. Leaving my body was a way to feel safe and to cut myself off from my feelings of dread. As a survival technique, I developed a highly responsible and perfectionist *good girl* self that operated out of my head. That served me in my childhood, but not as I aged and matured.

Along with my anxiety, I was also blessed with courage that allowed me to often override my anxiety. While feeling the fear, I did whatever it was anyway—drive, fly, meet new people, go to an interview for a new job, cook a new recipe, or decide for myself what to wear. Despite being able to push through, the constant presence of fear and judgment kept me small, always striving to get it right and feeling intimidated, which prevented me from feeling the joy and delight of my life.

My journey has been to come back into my body, where I can embrace my source of confidence and inner knowing. I have learned to listen deeply, trust my inner wisdom, and be guided by it. I now know how to embody, believe, and feel that I am good enough and that I have a place in this world. I have learned how to receive and know there is a deeper Source that supports me. I am now able to live joyfully out of my passion for teaching this freedom to others.

I continue to overcome the obstacles anxiety presents in my life by maintaining a connection to my body and inner wisdom, no matter what. I trust the messages I receive, and I act on them.

I heard early on in my healing journey that the most selfless act is to take care of yourself first, so you can take care of others and be present for them. While my desire to heal others led me to many amazing teachers, mentors, modalities of healing, and incredible experiences, it was showing up for myself and doing the hard inner work of healing— despite my resistance—that has allowed me to share what I do today.

My focus now is to help heal our planet by bringing individuals out of their heads and back into their own bodies. I help them embrace and trust their own inner wisdom, to know how to love, care, and advocate for themselves, so they can do the same for another.

The Body Centered Method evolved from many years of deep commitment to my own process and to healing others. Over time, I have become more embodied, allowing me to live and breathe from the core of my being. I have calmed my nervous system by silencing the critical, judgmental monkey mind, which is still present, but it does not have the same hold. While my anxiety is not totally gone, I have dominion over it, so it does not rule my life anymore.

I remain dedicated to my own healing, allowing layer by layer to reveal itself and peel away. The process has become a positive feedback loop, providing important information within the layers.

My passion, my calling, is as a healer. When I was younger, I had visions of being famous, being on TV, and speaking to large crowds. In fact, in my late 20s, I sat with my dearest boarding school friend on a small beach island in Sydney Harbour. We were doing a meditation prayer focused on our desire to be experts in our fields, well-known, and respected. I believe we have both achieved these things in different ways.

My vision of success is different now. It comes from knowing my own self, resting into my core, and surrendering to the oneness that connects me to the earth, the world, and the universe.

- My success now comes from knowing my voice, what I want, and learning to ask  for it in a trusting and loving way.
- My success now comes from opening to Source, from feeling an ever-present love, support, and guidance, and to know that I am not alone.
- My success now comes from knowing the difference between comfortably being by myself and the deep loneliness that separation and anxiety brings.

- My success now comes from sharing my experiences and my gifts with clients, friends, and family.
- My success now comes from learning to surrender, to accept, to forgive, and to be present in the reality of this moment.
- My success now comes from letting go of the fallacy of thinking everything was *my* fault, and that I was responsible.

Success for me is about inducing deep transformational healing in others so they can find and embrace the freedom I now know.

I have experienced loss, grief, disappointment, and trauma. However, by living within my body and deeply experiencing myself, I have been able to embrace them with dignity, courage, kindness, and love.

My biggest wish is for all beings to realize that becoming more embodied allows access to a treasure trove of internal wisdom. When someone longs for a better life, I know how the body's wisdom can be a critical partner to help that person resolve pain physically, mentally, or emotionally and to get *unstuck* from some life situation that is holding that person trapped or immobilized.

Through my own experience, I have learned that this is only possible if you take time for yourself first and reach out for the support you need. The process of taking the time to listen deeply to your inner voice can be uncomfortable, and resistance is likely to raise its grumbling head, but I have found that the results are always deeply rewarding.

Witnessing my clients learn how to trust in their life force from deep within and take their lives back has had a profound effect on me personally. This includes watching them become more present, more flexible, more trusting, and learning to *go with the flow.*

It also includes seeing them being more fluid in transitions between situations, thereby being less triggered by their emotions, and not getting lost in someone else's drama; as well as, becoming more resilient, staying more centered, and connected to their truth. Watching my clients share their feelings and convey their needs has been awe-inspiring.

I deeply appreciate that through my own healing, I have been able to empower, support, encourage, and hold the hands of many souls as they have realized a more joyful, free, and authentic life.

I have had a very rich life despite my fears. One of my mentors calls me *The Wisdom Messenger* because she sees my deeply intuitive nature and how I turn up and hold space for my clients, friends, and family. My mentor witnesses how much joy it brings me to live in my true authentic self. By holding that space of safety, my heart is filled and nourished to support others to shine their light, vibrate essential healthiness, happiness, and inclusiveness; and most of all, feel the love that is there for them.

At 60 years old, I am deeply thankful for the me I have embraced and become through my own adversity.

## About Tarnie

Tarnie Fulloon Israelsson is the creator of the Body Centered Method, a somatic healing practice that uncovers the messages held in the body resulting from past traumas, including challenging childhood and later-life experiences.

Tarnie's expertise lies in exploring the inner landscape for answers to the trauma held in the body: reoccurring pain, multiple body symptoms, anxiety, and places one feels *stuck* in their life.

Tarnie is a Body-Centered Method facilitator, mentor, speaker (Tedx Presenter), and author. Tarnie is honored to partner with those committed to their healing on all levels—physically, emotionally, mentally, and spiritually—and to empower them to be grounded and feel safe in their body to live a fulfilling life.

She lives with her physicist husband, Ulf, a lifelong seeker of spirituality. Their sacred retreat is their beautiful home in Altadena, Los Angeles, where Tarnie has a garden studio she enjoys working from.

**Connect with Tarnie**

www.tarniefulloon.com

tarnie@tarniefulloon.com

# Yes, I Can! Yes, You Can! Yes, We Can!

## Vickie Jones

"If you can't fly, then run. If you can't run, then walk. If you can't walk, then crawl. But whatever you do, you have to keep moving forward."[24]

- Dr. Martin L. King, Jr.

At 62 years old—a mother of 14 children, grandmother of 54 grandchildren, and great grandmother of one great-grandchild, *and* pastor of a church in the inner-city of Erie, Pa., with my husband, Bishop Curtis L. Jones Sr.—I was not sure about this new venture. My husband always wanted a store and a restaurant, which is great, but he does not cook (hmm). He has a

---

[24] King, Martin L. Jr. Speech at Spelman College, Spelman College Museum, April 1960, p.10-11

friend who opened a couple of restaurants; they collaborated, and initially, I just went along for the ride.

A restaurant seemed like a fun idea, if we had started earlier in life, but at 62, I was not convinced. However, the more my husband talked, the more the idea began to grow. A restaurant owned by blacks would be a positive statement in our community.

I have been in a church environment all my life, have a strong faith, and I am not afraid of hard work. The more I thought about it, my excitement began to catch up with my husband's and I found myself thinking, *let's get the show on the road!* We began but did not figure in a pandemic! So, now what?

We felt led by God to move forward despite what looked like a dismal business future. We worked tirelessly, especially my husband, to create a spot downtown. The location had been marked as a nuisance and shut down due to a stabbing, sadly taking the life of a young black male. An article in the Erie Times News explained the shutdown.[25] We decided we could turn this location's negative history into a positive, wonderful, and inviting place.

---

[25] City shuts down scene of fatal stabbing, Tim Hahn, April 30, 2019, https://www.goerie.com/story/news/crime/2019/04/30/city-shuts-down-scene-fatal/5291977007/

Born and raised in Erie, the goal was to create a safe, comfortable, exciting restaurant where you could get the best soul food and seafood imaginable. I am so grateful to my children who never doubted us and came together to help. Some of my children work at the restaurant, some live out of town and invested, and others did not get on board, but most of the 14 joined in. One thing that helped us keep hope and determination alive is our faith in God. Mark 9:23 reads, "Jesus said unto him, if thou canst believe, all things are possible to him that believeth."[26] So, in spite of the difficulties of opening a business, being African American, having very little money, a full-blown pandemic, and our lead cook contracting COVID-19 and missing the opening, we did it!

Our intention is for Chippers restaurant to be a beacon of light in our Erie community, the worst city for Black Americans to live in, according to 24/7 Wall Street. The article claimed, "No major metropolitan area has greater racial inequalities across major social and economic outcome measures than Erie."[27] My mom's dad was a chef and noted as one of the best cooks in southern Georgia. It is said, he cooked the food, but a white man's face was put on the label.

---

[26] Mark 9:23 (KJV)

[27] The Worst Cities for Black Americans, Evan Comen, Michael B. Sauter, November 3, 2017, https://247wallst.com/special-report/2017/11/03/the-worst-cities-for-black-americans-2/3/

Why name the restaurant "Chippers"? A friend of ours had a restaurant called "Chippers," which I thought was a silly name, but it made me chuckle and I realized it had a happy ring to it. It made me think of birds chirping, laughter, and good times. One day a guy came in and asked, "Did you guys name this restaurant 'Chippers' because everyone is so happy here? Every time I come in, I am greeted with smiles, laughter, and a big, 'Welcome to Chippers!'" This warmed my heart, because if we can make our customers' day a little brighter, hopefully, they will pay it forward. We have expanded the restaurant, building a stage for live music, poetry night, and more. We are adding a novelty shop for souvenirs, other trinkets, and a window for summer soft serve ice cream cones. Our menu is both seafood and southern cooking. You can get crab, shrimp, and fish, fried chicken with collard greens, and other delights.

During the worst of the pandemic, when everything was unsure—meet in person or home school; go to the office or work from home; open or close businesses; masks at home or just in public; open the church or go virtual; use Lysol, hand sanitizers, gloves, bleach, alcohol, peroxide, air purifiers; vaccinate or not; gather for holidays or FaceTime; curbside, door dash, or Uber eats—we persevered through it all. Three of my grown children and my husband contracted COVID-19. I am so grateful they all recovered. My heart and my condolences go out to lost loved ones and friends. Through all of this, we felt the urge to keep moving forward. I must admit, for a moment, I wasn't confident, but my husband never wavered. No matter how dark the darkness is, always believe in the light at the end of the tunnel. We believed in the light long before we saw it, and it's called faith!

As much as I love cooking, I was still not positive about opening a restaurant; however, we believe this inspiration was from God. He is bigger and greater than a pandemic or anything else standing in our way. With employee and family COVID-19 cases, fluctuating orange-yellow zones determining the number of people allowed to dine in at one time, we opted to do take out. *Wow!* Looking back today, it is a lot to take in, and we have to give God the credit for our ability to work through it all.

Our church went solely to online services and every Sunday we still got dressed for it and were visible online. We live-streamed from the church with our praise team and musicians, so we could still have praise and worship, a word given, and enjoy the presence of the Lord while being masked up and the air filled with Lysol. For the restaurant, it was take-out only, keeping a six-foot distance from others and adhering to mask mandates. This is *not* how we envisioned our grand opening, but it all worked out.

Here we are in 2022 and expanding seating capacity from 30 to 80 people. God is truly amazing. We have recently reopened the church, requiring much preparation to provide clean and safe in-person services.

During all this, we were planning a large wedding renewal ceremony to celebrate our 45th wedding anniversary. We had quite a few things in place, but those plans came to a screeching halt along with my youngest daughter's wedding plans. The pandemic certainly changed many plans and taught us how to be flexible and accept the things we cannot change.

Every once in a while, I get a glimpse of the fact that I am great because God within me is great, and I can say it with humility and heart. The beautiful thing about being 62 is the wisdom that allows me to see this. I found the courage to say *yes* to sharing and taking part in the anthology book. I said *yes*, to making new friends. *Yes,* is a powerful word and is opening up new and even greater things for me.

I told my eldest child about this anthology book and how it was taking me out of my comfort zone. His response was that I have to expand the zone that I am comfortable in. Great advice from son to mother. He is 100% right. There comes a moment when you simply step out, throwing caution to the wind!

When stepping out, you do not get to call the shots, but you do get to experience them. I've heard it said that life is a journey; indeed, it is. Every year that I have been graced to live has had its challenges, but the ability to be resilient is a gift from God. I have lost my dad, my mom, my sister, and my son, but somehow, I continue on life's journey. I love life. I am able to rise above coming from some dark places. I lost my fourth-born son to SIDS (crib death). He was three days from turning three months old. We were devastated. He was a beautiful and perfectly healthy baby boy. Even today, this haunts me.

The spirit of resiliency is crucial because life certainly has trials and tribulations. The spirit of resiliency is reflected in the food we serve, in the way it is served, and in the overall atmosphere of the restaurant. Our hearts' desire is that Chippers Seafood and Southern Fusion be more than just a place to get great food. We hope the experience blesses your body, soul, and spirit, so you get a sense of *Yes, you can! Yes, we can!* A sense that with God all things really are possible.

Martin Luther King Jr. said, "If you can't fly then run, if you can't run then walk, if you can't walk then crawl, but whatever you do, you have to keep moving forward." [28]

---

[28]

https://www.courierpostonline.com/story/opinion/readers/2018/01/12/commentary-fly-run-walk-crawl-advance-mlks-vision/1029899001/

## About Vickie

Vickie is a proud mother of 14 natural-born children (nine boys and five girls), grandmother of 54 grandchildren, and 1 great-grandchild. She has worked in various sectors including home health care, outpatient therapy services, community outreach programs, instructor for women's prison reentry programs/ministry, and currently serves as pastor for New Life and Spirit Revival Center in Erie, Pa., where her husband, the honorable Curtis L Jones Sr. is the bishop. These attributes have made her into the powerful woman she is today.

For many years, Vickie's life journey has groomed her personally and professionally to lead and guide others with an admirable passion, wisdom, and true confidence. Vickie is not only a pastor but also an entrepreneur, as she and her husband own Chippers Seafood and Southern Fusion restaurant. Opening a restaurant during the pandemic brought its challenges but ultimately became one of the things she is most proud of.

Her personal goal is both spiritual and natural. She believes without a doubt that spiritual food is good for the soul and natural food is good for nourishing the body. Vickie loves people and desires to bring out the best in herself while making a difference in many lives. Being a people person affords her the wonderful privileged to serve wherever she is needed most. There is not a moment when Vickie is not serving; however, in her downtime, she loves a nice manicure and being with family, cherishing every moment.

**Connect with Vickie**

PastorVickieJones@gmail.com

Facebook: Vickie Jones

# *Because I Knew You ...*

## Janet Kassir

"I don't ask for the sights in front of me to change, only the depth of my seeing."

*- Mary Oliver*

At a much younger age I was of the mindset that I could single handedly save the world. Have you ever had such thoughts? I also thought that the Blessed Virgin Mary was going to appear to me like she did to the children of Fatima in Portugal. Ugh! Let's get back to saving the world. What exactly was I saving the world from? Maybe from famine, malnutrition—I'm not sure—maybe it came from my mom telling me to eat everything on my plate because there were starving children in Africa. I just had this feeling I could do so much good and would make such a difference. And by the way, I did as I was told and ate everything on my plate.

As a result of the fire burning in my heart, I made it my mission to become a Peace Corps volunteer. I took the job offer in central Africa. Long story short, in the late 1970s, after a night of gathering with other Peace Corps volunteers, I started walking back to the embassy, when shocking events—surely not in the realm of this small-town girl's imagination—began to unfold. I was a naïve idealist neglecting any and all pragmatic interpretation of what was taking place around me. Before my eyes, the military tanks and locals wielding guns occupied the streets. Screams of a revolution were all but silenced by the crashing destruction of everything and anything that lay in their path. An actual coup d'état (overthrow of government) was in progress in the streets of the city of Bangui, the capital of the Central African Empire.

The absolute monarchy, under the dictatorship of a self-proclaimed Emperor Bokassa, was in the initial phase to oust him from power. Unfortunately, I happened to be in Bangui to get supplies and hoping to go back en brousse (back up country) as soon as it was possible, but this thing called revolution held me hostage. Don't worry, I was rescued off the streets by a French man who stopped in his vehicle and asked me what I was doing, why, and where I thought I was going. It ended up being a good idea to jump into the car with this unknown man—a thing I was taught never to do, along with eating everything on my plate—but at this moment it seemed like the only choice I had. I ended up at his home with his welcoming family. We savored a wonderful dinner, and you know the French and their wine, so of course wine; we had lots of wine. When all was safe to be on the streets once again, I headed back to the embassy safe at last!

Lessons I learned:

1. I could not save the world!
2. The Blessed Virgin Mary does not always appear.
3. I was the one who came out of this cross-cultural experience with the most gained, having learned to speak a foreign language, drive a motorcycle, dig a latrine, clean a water source, and of course barter for food at the market.
4. Malaria is no joke. Don't forget to take your anti-malaria medicine.
5. Being alone is a good thing. I learned to love the person I was and became comfortable in my own skin.
6. Use your alone time to learn and practice yoga and meditation.
7. US Foreign aid doesn't always get to the people who really need it.
8. Naiveté can get you through some dangerous times.
9. I was living in a bubble, knowing nothing about the politics of the outside world.
10. I do believe in love at first sight.

Fast forward about a year and a half later, in 1980, I found myself driving through one of the most gorgeous landscapes I'd ever seen. The blue Mediterranean Sea and white sands, mountains speckled with villas and palm trees, olive trees, and any kind of citrus tree you could imagine lay on the horizon. Quaint villages, delicious food, fragrant scents, and beautiful people were everywhere. Aside from the road-checks by men dressed in military garb and carrying machine guns, it was a picture of serenity. This landscape held no evidence of the hellish punishment experienced by all who lived in this conflicted war-torn country called Lebanon.

It was an evening like all the others as we sat on the veranda with my husband—love at first sight guy—and my new Lebanese family. All at once, an explosion ripped through the darkness and all one could hear was the loud ringing in your ears and the muffled screams; screams in a foreign language I did not understand. All I could see through the smoke were shadows of my family members finding their way to safety.

These mind-blowing and life-changing experiences shaped and defined the following days, months, and years of my life. Subconsciously, the shift and chemical changes occurred immediately. Consciously, it was a process, a self-reckoning of how my past changed me physically and emotionally. Noises that at one time were an afterthought or never caught my attention would make me run out of my house any time of the day or night as though it was a matter of life or death. These reactions to loud noises, like planes and helicopters, presented themselves over the next 30 years. These side effects of trauma reared their ugly head and were only more bearable after seeking professional help. Throughout the following years I carried on raising my precious family trying to subdue the anxiety caused by uncontrollable fear that could paralyze me at any given moment.

I'm like most women who help to raise a family and experience a roller coaster of events. This is life—we flow with the changes, continue to work, and keep a home. Our dreams are put on hold or somehow become pliable to fit everyone else's plans. My focus was to shine the light on our children and see to it that their dreams were realized. I soon found I was not the authority on everything I believed myself to be, not the one responsible for all the ideal outcomes in everyone's lives. Hooray! It was not my life's purpose to protect my family from the struggles nor guarantee the successes. I know many women have this revelation, waking one day and wondering what happened to me? Where did I go? Where is that fun loving, full of life and luster, fearless woman? How was my identity so easily lost and how did I end up last on my own list of to dos?

After many years of neglecting the need to resurrect that fun loving proponent of a healthier, more spiritual me, I finally surfaced. I had been operating under the guise of what I expected myself to be as a parent, wife, and woman. I only wish that I had listened to my inner voice and made time for myself to breathe sooner. I was finally breathing in the much-needed care, attention, love, and forgiveness I was entitled to. Opening my heart and spirit to the Universe, raising my energy to a higher level of transformation; transcending the fear, negativity, and malfunction of (my ego), and having the power to overcome it was vital to me. I'm grateful for all of the growth that I have encountered through life's blessings, lessons, and hardships.

My latest venture started about 12 years ago. It was not something I had dreamed of or even wished for. Motivated by a relocation to a new city, I knew I needed to reach out into the community and make friends. I knew I had to think outside of the box for a new and unique business. I chose a product that had a lot of meaning to me and jumped in feet first—scarves! Simply Scarves-Tie One On, was the name of my business for years, it recently evolved into its new name, Boutique N Bling with Janet Kassir. The business grew from scarves to ponchos, purses, hats, and now jewelry, and various other accessories. My inspiration each day is the passion and joy I feel when I see a customer looking at themselves in the mirror and experiencing that ah-ha moment as they love what they see looking back at them. It gives me a thrill that my products create such an amazing, positive reaction in someone's life, if not just for that moment.

Here are ten suggestions for you my dear readers to enable yourselves to reach your full potential.

1. Dig deep to overcome your fears. Ask for help, meditate, medicate (if you need to) but reconnect with your fearless self so you can experience all that you desire to do and be.
2. Surround yourself with like-minded women. I still remember the day I walked into a meeting of all women entrepreneurs. It was like I had been sent a gift from the Universe. This particular networking group was founded by Heidi Parr Kerner in Erie, Pa., called The Coffee Club Divas. Do yourself a favor and find your tribe.

3. Move your body. I should do more of this!

4. Make a plan of action every day. Write it out on a calendar, a notebook, or your cell phone, and check it off as you accomplish each task on your list. Create short and long-term challenges. You need to wake with a purpose and a focus to your day.

5. Make lunch plans with women you trust to be in your space and who you are willing to spend valuable time talking, laughing, and sharing.

6. Make time for the most valuable person in your life—*you*. Meditate, watch a great movie, read, walk, start writing that book you've always dreamed of. Take care of your heart, so that it's not aching; take care of your thoughts, so that they are not harmful; take care of your body so that it will serve you; and lastly take care of your spirit so it will lift you up.

7. Share, give, compliment, help, pray, forgive.

8. Practice gratitude. Be grateful, be grateful, be grateful!

9. If you can't do it alone, ask for help. Not all of us are social media gurus, computer geeks, or financial advisors. We are the creative ones, the savvy entrepreneurs who love to share our business and thrive as a result.

10. Now that your kids have grown and are not the needy, time suckers they once were, (ha!) enjoy them, they have much to offer and will most likely be your best friends. They can be extremely funny and a reflection of yourself.

Encourage them not to leave behind those fun loving, fearless, adventurous selves they once were.

I have shared with you two of the most significant events in my 60 and beyond years on this planet. Even though I have given you a number of significant lessons learned, I'm sure there are many more. I will sum it all up with a quote from a song that has much meaning to me, and I hope it will for you as well.

"For Good"

"I've heard it said
That people come into our lives for a reason
Bringing something we must learn
And we are led
To those who help us most to grow
If we let them
And we help them in return
Well, I don't know if I believe that's true
But I know I'm who I am today
Because I knew you [...]"

"I have been changed for the better...because I knew you.[29]"

———————————————

[29] Schwartz, Stephen. "For Good." Wicked. https://www.lyricsondemand.com/soundtracks/w/wickedlyrics/iknewyoulyrics.html

Because I knew you ... I'm stronger, I'm weaker, I'm kinder, I'm meaner, I'm more hopeful, I'm discouraged, I'm proud, I'm shameful, I'm angry, I'm happy, I'm satisfied, I'm uninspired, I'm motivated, I'm fearful, I'm brave. It is up to me to take from my encounters the best and learn from the worst.

Finally, I must admit that my current older and wiser mindset, is not thinking I can save the world, as my younger self did. However, I am resilient. I am relighting the fire in my heart that burns to live an extraordinary life with the coming of each new day and welcoming all its new challenges, journeys, and unexpected life-changing moments.

**About Janet**

Founder of Boutique N Bling with Janet Kassir—formally Simply Scarves-Tie One On—a fun and fashion-filled e-accessory business with pop-up shops that delight those hands-on clients. Her perfect blend of charismatic appeal and creative style succeeds in bringing stylish new trends and classic fashions to women of all ages. Janet helps her clients to experience that ah-ha moment when they look in the mirror and love what they see! Janet previously owned and managed The Option House, an eating and drinking establishment, and a florist shop called Bloomers with her husband, the love at first sight guy of 43 years. Mother of three and grandmother of two grandsons, she lives to love fiercely with each new day.

**Connect with Janet**

www.boutiquenbling.com

https://www.facebook.com/janetkassirtieoneon

Boutique N Bling with Janet Kassir

# *Footloose and Fancy-Free*

## Peggy Schwab

"Your second life begins when you realize you only have one."[30]

- Raphaëlle Giordano

I stood on my grandfather's size 12 shoes at age three and learned the Jitterbug. Daddy Bob introduced me to dance, and I haven't stopped since. I remember something magical happening; I felt the music in my body, and I liked it! I was so young at the time that I did not realize I was creating lifetime memories. Some of my earliest memories are of staring up at Daddy Bob and seeing his smiling face as he simultaneously danced and balanced his first granddaughter standing on his feet. I have two younger sisters, so it's safe to say my grandfather had many years of blisters and a regimen of ice and aspirin. I'm almost certain he wouldn't have had it any other way!

---

[30] Giordano, Raphaëlle. Penguin Random House,
https://www.penguinrandomhouse.com/authors/2170201/raphaelle-giordano/

One could say I was *born to move*. From the ages of five to 15, I studied dance and participated inballet, tap, and hard-toe recitals. Cheerleading in middle school wasn't particularly my cup of tea; however, high school introduced the opportunity to become a majorette. I thoroughly enjoyed allfour years twirling and tossing my baton in the house, the hallways at school, and of course in line up with my dance team.

Growing up in Kimberly, W.Va., my parents, Bette and Don Kincaid, had their hands full raising three daughters: Peggy, Pam, and Penny, the original PPP. My dad was surrounded by females, a much different environment than the one he envisioned for many years. He was determined to have boys. In fact, each basinet included a baseball, exemplifying his confidence and premonitions of a son: *first pitch, strike one, welcome Peggy to the world. Second pitch, strike two, welcome Pamela. It's now or never Don. You're down in the count but your continued confidence has proven impressive. The stage is set—swing and a miss—Penny's first appearance, strike three.*

In retrospect, my dad fully realized the stereotypical male adolescent scenarios that often accompany a boy's journey toward manhood, except they were played out with me! I climbed trees and had scraped knees consistently for the first ten years of my life. I baited my male cousin's hooks with worms when we'd go fishing because they were "too ewwy" for him. Best of luck to anyone getting him to make any admissions to this very day. My dad received phone calls from school upon occasion requesting to pick up his first-born daughter, she's beating up the boys at recess.

My beautiful younger sister, Pamela, was perfectly behaved, a cherub one could say. She never wanted to rock the boat, and it's a good thing because I think I made my dad plenty seasick.

Penny provided an impressive performance herself, putting a tumultuous bow on the Kincaid childhood. My mother swore that Penny was the reincarnation of me; and Pamela, like the calm eye of a hurricane, gave them a much-needed opportunity to catch their breath and regroup, fully aware of the catastrophe nearing the shore. After graduation, I decided to pursue physical education as a career and attended West Virginia Tech. After three semesters, I decided on a whim to enroll in Juliet Gibson Career College for Women in Covington, Ky., right across the bridge from Cincinnati, Ohio. It was there I was thrown another curveball. It was brought to my attention that American Airlines was holding interviews at the Cincinnati Airport; hopping in a taxi, off I went! I left, not even looking back.

The opportunity to become a stewardess in 1970 (better known today as flight attendant) was a very sought-after and exclusive position. This was a deviation from my life plan, but I couldn't resist. What better way to travel and experience other parts of the country? Growing up in wild, wonderful West Virginia was certainly as John Denver advertised, yet I still had a desire to spread my wings and fly. (No pun intended. OK, maybe just a little.) First, I must interview and compete against hundreds and hundreds of applicants. The following represents the interview in order and in entirety:

- First, I was asked to get on a scale.
- Second, they measured my hips.
- Third, they measured my height.
- Last, I was asked my name.

That was it. In today's world it's almost incomprehensible, but it was a different time. How times have changed! Honestly, the interview quickly became an afterthought, and I continued my coursework at school. That is until about ten days later when my parents received a letter congratulating their oldest daughter for being selected to work for American Airlines! Immediately, I was to report to Dallas, Tex., for six weeks of training. *No*, my parents hadn't the slightest clue I had been interviewed; and *yes*, they knew before I did! Fortunately, they were quite supportive given the situation. Without any time to reflect or object, I began my journey to the Lonestar State.

My training was complete, and I was assigned to a station in New York City for the next two years.

The experience was one I wouldn't trade for the world. I was born to move and move we did. From gate to gate and city to city, each day was a nonstop, action-packed schedule. Early morning wake-up calls and late-night taxi rides to and from the airport motels didn't leave much time to eat, shower, and get a few hours of sleep before we were up and preparing to do it all again. I must admit it was a rush, but more importantly, the experience granted me a newfound perspective and solidified my desire to return to school.

Upon returning home from New York, I was anxious to settle back into academia; however, life decidedly threw me another curveball. I met my very handsome husband, and Kerry and I are about to celebrate our 50th wedding anniversary this June. The first day we met, he boasted to his best friend, "I'm going to marry that girl." Knowing nothing about Erie, even with all my travels, I remember asking him, "Kerry, you're from where? Erie, Pa.?" There were many occasions when flying that I was unsure of what city we were in, but I'm almost positive Erie was not one of them. Little did I know, a city three hundred miles due north would become the place I call home. Erie was a place that grew on me as I grew in it over the years.

We settled in, enjoying each other's company and the nuances of marriage. I greatly cherish this time in my life, and looking back now, I realize how much credit must be attributed to the foundation we built during this time. 50 years of marriage seems surreal, as just yesterday we were plotting our future. We both wanted children eventually, so when opportunity arose, we traveled as much as we could. Kerry's family loved to travel, and I did not have the chance to truly enjoy most of the remarkable places I visited while with the airlines. Our travels included

Germany, Austria, Italy, the Hawaiian Islands, boating adventures up and down the Great Lakes, and my personal favorite, a trip to the Left Coast, sunny Palm Springs, Ca. It was there I was approached by a gentleman with eyes every bit as blue as the Pacific, Frank Sinatra. Mr. Sinatra asked if I was married and before I could answer, my six-foot four-inch handsome husband replied, "Yes, she is ... and happily." We still laugh about the run-in today.

It wasn't but a couple of years of living in Erie when my world changed forever. Losing my Daddy Don at the age of 64 was utterly devastating. I had two young sons and my dad had eagerly awaited the opportunity to dust off the footballs and restring the fishing poles in the distinguished capacity of grandfather. Sadly, my dad and my boys never had the chance to enjoy one of life's finest treasures, the bond created between grandparents and grandchildren. My mom, known asMema, now a widow at the young age of 60, became a realtor to pass the time. She enjoyed her work and within a few short years graduated to the position of broker. Pam, Penny, and I were so proud of her, yet heartbroken. Living in Erie at the time, I found strength in my mom's resilience and took a page from her playbook. The kids were still very young, so much of my time was accounted for, but I did find a way to begin selling Mary Kay cosmetics. I had much success for a number of years, up until my sons were old enough to go to school.

At the time, Kerry's parents were hotel owner-operators, and he made the decision to join the family's business. His father had been a longstanding pharmacist and owned a pharmacy on the outskirts of downtown Erie. After returning home from World War II, he felt he was missing Kerry's, and younger daughter Candy's, childhoods. The pharmacy occupied too much time and Kerry's parents made the bold decision to sell the business and purchase a small motel with the proceeds. Without any previous experience in the hospitality field, his parents learned from the ground up. Perhaps the greatest realization was the 24-hour, 7-days-a-week operating cycle. At least the pharmacy closed in the late evening till the next morning. Kerry worked long hours as the Schwab family slowly grew and expanded their business. Often, our two sons, KJ and Travis, hoped to catch a glimpse of Dad before the morning school bus or with just enough daylight remaining for a quick game of catch in the backyard. Born just 18 months apart, I believe my time with the airlines provided me the stamina to keep up with our two sons.

When the kids were old enough to go to school, I found I had some time during the day and began to teach an aerobics class three times a week at a gym called Nautilus, completely unaware I would still be teaching there today, 36 years later. Although today it's known as Fitness U. Over time, I found myself teaching five days a week and as the months and years passed, I acquired multiple certifications for the ever-changing trends in the fitness world. Aerobics in the 1980s was replaced by step-aerobics, and then Tae Bo became the overwhelming fad. Most recently, Zumba, and other variations have dominated instructor-led group classes. I have taught them all, establishing a tremendous and loyal following. It is through my exercise classes that I have developed the most incredible group of friends. For those 36 years, I've been fortunate to begin each day by spending a couple of hours with those that I will forever cherish. I've gone back and forth in my mind about retirement, but as long as my peeps continue to show up, I will as well.

One of my passions, in addition to dance and exercise, has always been women's fashion. I owned and operated a boutique dress shop for 20 years, Four Seasons by Peggy. I traveled back to New York City four or five times a year to buy for the store. The fashion industry is fast-paced and constantly evolving as trends come and go throughout the seasons. I found the business to be a very challenging but rewarding experience. I was fortunate to work with an extremely special group of clients.

My sons, KJ and Travis, moved away from home to attend college, and I needed something to occupy the time I had spent with them the previous 20 years. I decided to rejoin the corporate world as a wedding planner at our family's full-service hotel, The Bel-Aire Hotel and Conference Center. I found my new position to be the culmination of all my life's undertakings: the infinite detail, organization of vendors, guest lists, menu and bar preparation, overnight accommodation arrangements, rehearsals, post-reception brunches, interdepartmental communications, invoice and accounting reconciliation, and my favorite, the relationships formed with the brides as their special day grew closer and closer to becoming a reality. In addition to this new undertaking, in 2019, I became a fashion director for another family-owned business known as Park Lane Jewelry. I relished my dual roles and was promoted to branch director in two years.

As previously mentioned, our family's livelihood is cultivated from decades-long hotel operations. For over 50 years and three generations, we have witnessed just about everything the hospitality industry and economic climate had to offer. Over time, roadside motels with exterior entrances became antiquated as larger hotels with more amenities and specialized features for patrons dominated new construction projects nationally. We adapted, and more importantly, anticipated such shifts. We experienced a surging demand for our products and services throughout the 1980s and the first half of the 1990s. Like all global commerce today, property management systems and marketing campaigns quickly digitized to take advantage of what the internet could provide.

9/11 was of course a detrimental and tragic blow to our country, yet hotels were especially affected for many years after. Traveler behavior and perception changed forever. We were slow to react and had to make what seemed to be at the time nearly impossible staffing and cultural adjustments. Fearing the inability to maintain our consistent customer service efforts, we came out leaner, more efficient, and smarter. This catastrophic event, which seemed at the time to be the end of the world, later proved to be the second worst economic event in the twenty-first century, the first being the financial collapse in 2008. After finally realizing some financial stability, the economic downturn resulting from the housing and stock market-driven recession changed the banking perception of hotels. Once viewed as a stable investment changed to high-risk, capital-intensive projects far less attractive in the eyes of lenders. Higher interest rate loans coupled with strict owner equity infusion and personal guarantees became reality for hotels fortunate enough to survive the Great Recession.

Our most challenging experience is our most recent, as all economic indicators, coupled with several years of increased revenue streams, pointed toward an anticipated ten-year high for the fiscal year of 2020. After several years of financial losses, we battled our way back into the marketplace and entered the 2020 year with a $1.6 million complete property renovation. We were fresh, competitively priced, and rejuvenated to recapture some of the markets we had lost to the competition and economic circumstances. The first quarter was proving to be even stronger than our forecast, then it happened ... Just like everyone else, we found ourselves in a pandemic that proved to be the most overwhelming professional and personal struggle our family had everencountered.

This time it felt different. Business ceased and future projections were simply unknown. Deemed an *essential* operation, we remained open throughout the pandemic and wouldn't have wanted it any other way. Each day posed new challenges and we weren't about to succumb to the most recent challenge. Stay positive, stay healthy, maintain strict COVID-19 protocols, and remain vigilant. Days became weeks and weeks became months. Accruing more debt to maintain daily operations resulted in a true reversal of early-year projections. Our business model is constructed to follow the overnight demand generators (sporting events, conventions, leisure, shopping, theme park and family vacations, weddings, family reunions, and other social events). These events were non-existent, not just deemed to be potential virus super spreaders for the masses, but mandated to close by authoritative and governmental agencies. The uncertainty of *if and when* life would return to normal presented extra stress on us all.

For over 50 years, our family glasses remained half full, regardless of the times, but for the first time, I could see the joy slip from the faces of Kerry and KJ. Removing emotion from business decisions has always been a requirement, yet not always a simple task when passion and drive consume one's lifelong journey. I suppose we all are driven by an internal music, some literally and some metaphorically. Although COVID-19 presented my family's longest slow dance, we've taken turns being Daddy Bob and have ultimately persevered.

I buried myself in Park Lane during the pandemic, determined to somehow continue building and maintaining relationships even at a drastically reduced capacity. We coordinated virtual shows and product introductions through Zoom. It was never really about selling, but simply the enjoyment of friendship and a much-needed escape from the realities everyday life presented during that time. Now that things have seemingly stabilized and a sense of normalcy once again lingers in the air, I am teaching and dancing during the day and shining like a star at night with my Park Lane Jewelry. *Bling it on Ladies!*

For now, I'll keep on dancing ...

## About Peggy

Photo by AR Treasures Photography

Peggy R. Schwab, a lifelong fitness guru, has continued to instruct and motivate others to *feel the burn* for over 30 years. She's well known for introducing Zumba to the Erie area in 2005 as a certified Instructor. Originally from the south, she grew up as the oldest of three girls. Peggy boasts an impressive array of sales experiences throughout her career. She is the owner of The Four Season's by Peggy, a women's luxury clothing boutique; the director of sales for her family's hotel operations; and the branch manager for Park Lane Jewelry. As a proud mother of two, her

210

professional accomplishments cannot compare to her personal ones; she and her husband most recently celebrated 50 years of marriage. According to her, family will always reign atop the list of life's greatest successes.

**Connect with Peggy**

peggy@schwabhospitality.com

parklanejewelry.com/peggyschwab

https://www.facebook.com/peggy.schwab.37

# Small Town Jewel

## Valerie Weaver

"Follow your passion. It will lead you to your purpose."

- Oprah Winfrey

Just a stone's throw from Cook Forest State Park sits a small, one-blinker town, Leeper, Pa. This is where my parents, Jim and Kitty Pfendler, raised me and my three siblings: Doug, Melissa, and Paula. Our close proximity to Cook Forest (known for camping and outdoor activities) made this an ideal place to start an RV business. Seeing my parents' business grow from two small RVs in our yard to becoming one of the largest dealers in western PA showed me early on that hard work, taking chances, and believing in yourself pay off.

My summers included working at the RV store and family-owned campground. Weekends were spent around campfires making mountain pies and telling stories. My parents made a great team – mom, with her big personality, and dad, the quiet, big-picture kind of guy. He was the master of pivoting when

213

challenges arose. I like to believe I inherited that gene. Looking back, I learned so much from them and attribute a great deal of my success to the invaluable lessons they taught me.

**Diamonds and Rough**

After high school, my siblings went off to college to pursue degrees while I decided to jump into the working world. My first job was at a bank in Clarion, Pa. I loved meeting new people and interacting with small business owners. I was always intrigued and thought *someday that could be me!*

In the winter of 1986, tragedy struck our family not once, but twice, in a matter of days. First, my uncle and his son were struck by a drunk driver and my uncle passed away from his injuries. The day after his funeral, my mother had a massive heart attack and died instantly.

She was only 54 years old. We were in shock and disbelief. One week, two funerals. It was surreal. Time stopped. Words ceased.

**Golden Opportunity**

After two tragic losses, I needed a change and began to assess my options. As fate would have it, the bank merged with one in Erie, Pa., and I applied for a transfer. A move was soon in place, and I was on my way to the *big city*. What a big change, but I was ready for the adventure.

The bank was an exciting place to work with many social activities and opportunities to meet new people. I enjoyed working as a teller and in new accounts, but I was always intrigued by the executive offices. When a position became available, I applied; even though I thought I may not be the most qualified and I landed the job.

**Hidden Gem:** Always go for the opportunity that is knocking

I assisted the executive secretary and one day, in her absence, the bank president asked me if I could "take a letter." I asked him where he wanted me to take it. We still laugh about that to this day!

One day while reading the newspaper I noticed an ad for an Image Consultant. I *loved* fashion so I inquired. It was a direct sales company, BeautiControl Cosmetics. They trained you to be an image consultant and market their skin care and cosmetic line.

I learned the direct sales (party plan) business model and that I would be paid based on my personal sales *and* commissions on anyone I recruited into the company. What an opportunity to merge my interest in small business *and* my love of fashion. I joined and did home parties marketing their products. Bank by day, image consultant by night. A perfect side hustle!

**A Fashionista is Born**

A few years later, our bank merged again, and my position was restructured to part-time. This gave me the opportunity to pursue my side hustle. In 1992, I took a leap of faith and ventured out on my own, pursuing sales full-time. Scary, yes, but I had the confidence to give it a shot and I was ready. At this same time, I joined Premier Designs Jewelry so I could offer women a complete line of products/services to help them look their best. I mean, no one leaves home without lipstick and earrings, and I had both to offer!

**Hidden Gem:** One of the biggest reasons people stay in a "safe zone" is because of the fear of failure and the unknown. Failure and success go hand in hand. You can't experience one without the other.

I focused on my jewelry home shows, and oh, the stories I could tell! Once I was greeted at the door by a sign *Jewelry lady just come in.* No hostess, just a room full of taxidermied deer heads. I immediately began to size up which earrings would look best on them! Then there was the time a rambunctious five-year-old grabbed a string of pearls and ran off to the bathroom — *whoosh* was the next sound I heard!

During this time, my image consulting business grew steadily. I attended the London Image Institute in Atlanta, Ga., became a certified image consultant, and created Premier Images. I marketed professional image programs and I remember lugging a projector, overheads, and a rack of clothes along with me!

**Hidden Gem:** As an entrepreneur, you always need to stay educated and have a teachable spirit. To experience continued success, you have to stay relevant in your field of expertise in this fast-paced world we live in.

Many doors began to open for me which led to exciting opportunities. I found the media world fascinating and was fortunate to become a part of it! I served as a TV representative for the Millcreek Mall, interviewing mall tenants for a weekly TV segment, *Focus On Style*. I became a guest on a weekly radio show, *Fashion Friday*, offering fashion tips to listeners. I also began writing a column for a local women's magazine, *Her Times*, and landed a segment on WJET-TV as their *Frugal Fashionista*. I still appear regularly on the Money Segment. This segment features experts offering valuable advice in their fields. As the *Frugal Fashionista*, I share money-saving tips on everything from fashion to entertaining.

**Hidden Gem:** Always be looking for new opportunities because they are everywhere. Be open-minded and make networking a priority.

In 1999, I accepted a position with Stein Mart as their community outreach fashion consultant. This included marketing the store through special events and wardrobing the local TV anchors. During this time, I was approached about a new direct sales company, Home and Garden Party. With my experience, I knew the business model well. This was a big change from my past products, but I knew women would love it. After joining, I started recruiting women to sell home decor products. The business grew by leaps and bounds and so did my income.

## Family Matters

Along the way, I met my future husband, Michael. He was a business owner himself and was very supportive of my career, as he also possessed that entrepreneurial spirit.

By 2005, we were planning a dream destination wedding on the beach in Riviera Maya, Mexico. I was so excited to have 34 friends and family coming together to share this intimate celebration. Two weeks before the wedding, Hurricane Wilma barreled through Mexico and devastated the resort. It had to be canceled—oh, the disappointment!

Our plans changed instantly. We met with our travel agent and rescheduled the event for three months later, so it all worked out. What memories!!

**Hidden Gem:** Stay calm. Get over disappointments quickly. Focus on what you **can** control, not what you can't.

In January 2010, my dad suffered a stroke and was unresponsive. My siblings and I all flew to Florida to be at his bedside. Within an hour, after we all arrived, a tear ran down his face and he took his last breath. It was so apparent that he waited for us.

We all returned to Leeper for his funeral and viewing. It was the largest funeral ever held in that tiny little town. Fire trucks directed traffic and the visitation lines were out the door. He truly was a beloved member of that community. What a moving tribute for a wonderful dad who taught all of us so much.

## Family Jewel

In 2011, the commission structure at Home and Garden Party changed and so would my income. I was truly at a crossroads. About this time, I received a call from a trusted colleague who I had worked with in the other direct sales companies. She shared her discovery of Park Lane Jewelry. Initially, I was hesitant, but out of courtesy I listened to her, and I agreed to an interview with a corporate executive. I was very impressed!

I learned that Park Lane Jewelry was founded in 1955 by Shirley and Art Levin. A family business that was being run by the second generation. Park Lane had so much to offer: a beautiful line of jewelry, stability, longevity, great commissions, incentive trips, and many other perks. They recognized my 22 years of experience, and I accepted their offer. I entered at a leader level. Game on!

Wow, what a great decision! For the next ten years, I excelled at in-home jewelry shows and hosted fun Sip & Style events at different venues. I rebuilt my team and was recognized as a consistent top seller, earning all the wonderful perks that came with it ... including 14 dream vacations to Spain, London, Paris, and more. I knew this was my wheelhouse.

**Hidden Gem:** Love what you do, and you will never work another day in your life

## Pandemic: Sink or Swim

In March of 2020, COVID-19 hit. My full schedule of jewelry shows and events were canceled. The entire country ground to a screeching halt as we went into lockdown. So now what?

I had many emotions: fear, panic, and disbelief. How was I going to survive? I was in the people business; this is what I knew and loved. Quitting was not an option.

Panic and uncertainty abounded. I soon got over the shock and I could hear my dad in my ear saying, "You will figure it out."

**Hidden Gem:** When challenges and obstacles arise, don't throw in the towel. Huge adversities may turn out to be a silver lining in the end.

## Sisters Unite

The Coffee Club Divas, a women's networking group I belong to, hosted a Zoom call soon after lockdown. It made me realize I wasn't alone. We put our heads together, supported one another, and began shifting our business models.

**Hidden Gem**: Think outside of the box and reach out for help when you need it.

I pivoted and began offering virtual Zoom style shows. Technology being a weakness for me, I enlisted the help of an assistant and focused on what I knew best—having fun presenting the jewelry.

**Hidden Gem:** Know your strengths and weaknesses and focus on what you do best. Learn to delegate and get assistance when needed.

During quarantine, I had a captive audience and learned a whole new skill set. I created Facebook groups for my hosts and learned how to do everything virtually experiencing many learning curves along the way. It was challenging, but I had others to learn from.

Going virtual actually expanded my host/customer reach from Florida to California. Sales exploded and so did my business.

**Hidden Gem:** Lean in and just do it. Don't overthink it.

I created a private Park Lane Sparkle & Style Facebook community for my hosts and customers. Going live daily allowed me to inspire, inform, and entertain the women with practical fashion advice and ideas including contests, giveaways, and exclusive sales. We became a virtual community. My audience was engaged and steadily grew as they enjoyed the distraction from the pandemic. This community has grown to over *650* women and it continues to be a mainstay of my business.

In May of 2021, I was back out in the world doing business like I had always done—in person. This time, bolder and wiser. This experience tested my mettle and made me dig deep. My faith, tenacity, and determination would not allow circumstances that were out of my control determine my destiny.

Above all, it has affirmed my motto:

Get up,

Dress up,

Show up,

and Never Give Up!

**Hidden Gem:** Always be willing to evolve and grow. It will be key to your success!

## About Valerie

Valerie Weaver is a certified image consultant through the London Image Institute in Atlanta, Ga. She has an extensive background in fashion and media spanning over 30 years. Valerie has served as the TV representative for the Millcreek Mall, appeared as a regular guest on STAR 104's weekly radio show *Fashion Friday*, and was a contributing columnist to the *Her Times* magazine.

In her role as an image consultant, she created and owned Premier Images, a professional image consulting business. She taught business etiquette, professional image, and non-verbal communication programs to various corporations.

Valerie is the personal stylist for influencers such as Patty Farmer, marketing & media speaker, podcast host and magazine publisher, and a 7-figure event producer. She is known as WJET-TV's Frugal Fashionista and is a regular guest on the "Your Money" segment, offering money-saving advice on everything from fashion to entertainment.

A senior division stylist with Park Lane Jewelry, she shares her fashion expertise to inspire women to discover and express their personal styles. Valerie is consistently recognized as a Top 50 Worldwide Sales Producers for Park Lane and regularly provides training programs at Park Lane's National Sales Conventions held bi-annually.

Valerie resides with her husband Michael and two fashionable felines in Erie, Pa.

**Connect with Valerie**

Style Community:
https://www.facebook.com/groups/375356816006426

www.valerieweaver.com

valerieweaver34@gmail.com

# Thank you!

The authors of *20 Lives Ignited* hope you've enjoyed our stories and feel inspired by our journeys.

We invite you to join us in creating success on our own terms at www.facebook.com/20livesignited.

CPSIA information can be obtained
at www.ICGtesting.com
Printed in the USA
LVHW081107031022
729831LV00012B/649